# AWAKENING BRILLIANCE
# IN THE WRITER'S
# WORKSHOP

### Using Notebooks,
### Mentor Texts,
### and the
### Writing Process

## Lisa Morris

EYE ON EDUCATION
6 DEPOT WAY WEST, SUITE 106
LARCHMONT, NY 10538
(914) 833–0551
(914) 833–0761 fax
www.eyeoneducation.com

Sponsoring Editor: Robert Sickles
Production Editor: Lauren Davis
Copyeditor: Melissa McDaniel
Designer and Compositor: Publishing Synthesis, Ltd.
Cover Designer: Knoll Gilbert
Cover Image: Sunrise, Anastasiya Igolkina/Shutterstock

**Library of Congress Cataloging-in-Publication Data**
Morris, Lisa, 1969–
  Awakening brilliance in the writer's workshop: using notebooks,
  mentor texts, and the writing process/Lisa Morris.
    p. cm.
  ISBN 978-1-59667-195-9

1. English language—Composition and exercises—Study and teaching
(Elementary)  2. Writers' workshops.  3. School notebooks.  I. Title.
LB1576.M785 2011
372.62'3—dc23
                                                    2011024946

10 9 8 7 6 5 4 3 2 1

# Also Available from Eye On Education

**Write With Me:**
**Partnering With Parents in Writing Instruction**
Lynda Wade Sentz

**Writer's Workshop for the Common Core:**
**A Step-by-Step Guide**
Warren E. Combs

**Active Literacy Across the Curriculum:**
**Strategies for Reading, Writing, Speaking, and Listening**
Heidi Hayes Jacobs

**Teaching Grammar:**
**What Really Works**
Amy Benjamin and Joan Berger

**Vocabulary at the Center**
Amy Benjamin and John T. Crow

**Family Reading Night**
Darcy Hutchins, Marsha Greenfeld, and Joyce Epstein

**Building a Culture of Literacy Month-by-Month**
Hilarie Davis

**Literacy Leadership Teams:**
**Collaborative Leadership for Improving and**
**Sustaining Student Achievement**
Pamela S. Craig

**Literacy from A to Z**
Barbara R. Blackburn

**Battling Boredom:**
**99 Strategies to Spark Student Engagement**
Bryan Harris

**101 Poems for Teachers**
Annette Breaux

**The Passion-Driven Classroom:**
**A Framework for Teaching and Learning**
Angela Maiers and Amy Sandvold

**Rigor is NOT a Four-Letter Word**
Barbara R. Blackburn

# Dedication

To my dear friend and principal, Shelly Arneson, who believed in me when I was not sure I had it in me. Though it is many years later, I still carry in my wallet the words of encouragement that she handed me one day on a little note card:

"Believe deep down in your heart that you are destined to do great things."
—Joe Paterno

# About the Author

Lisa Morris teaches language arts at Edge Elementary in Niceville, Florida. She has been an educator for 21 years. She also conducts writing workshops for the teachers in her district. Lisa holds a master's degree in early childhood education from Lagrange College. She was nominated as the 2009–2010 Teacher of the Year at her current school.

Lisa has published personal stories in *Chicken Soup for the Soul*, magazine articles for *Just Labs* magazine, and two thematic teaching units for Frank Schaffer Publications. She currently serves as the president of the Gulf Coast Writers Guild. Lisa also devotes her time to her four Labrador retrievers and two children, Katie Marie and Bella Grace.

# Contents

# Free Downloads

Extended versions of the mentor text lists and quote lists that appear on pages 186 and 191 of this book are available on Eye On Education's Web site as Adobe Acrobat files. Permission has been granted to purchasers of this book to download these resources and print them.

You can access these downloads by visiting Eye On Education's Web site: www.eyeoneducation.com. Click FREE DOWNLOADS or search or browse our Web site to find this book, and then scroll down for downloading instructions.

You'll need your book buyer access code: AWB-7195-9.

# Introduction

All educators have moments in their careers when they know they have truly made a difference. These moments do not come daily, and sometimes they are scattered far in between, but they are what keep us going. These are the moments that lift our spirits in times of budget cuts, standardized testing, and curricular demands. In the 2008–2009 school year, my fourth-grade students and I accepted a challenge to be the best writers we could and produce the highest writing scores ever. We accomplished that task. This was one of those moments for me. The writing standards for our state test had become more academically challenging, and we were struggling. My principal asked me to departmentalize that year and teach language arts to all the fourth graders. Now, I adore my principal (we are very close), and there isn't much I wouldn't do for her, but taking on the task of teaching and being responsible for all of the writing was, to say the least, a little overwhelming. Taking on this task would mean I had the state writing results looming over my head. I certainly had my doubts at first. I had worked hard to improve my teaching of writing, and my confidence was blossoming, yet this would be a task unlike any I had taken on before. But if she had that much confidence in me, I would give it a try.

I moved to the area I now call home six years ago. It was one of the best decisions of my life. When I first entered the front door of my current school, I knew I was where I was supposed to be. My first job at this school was a third-grade teaching position. I enjoyed the curriculum and formed a strong bond with my fellow teachers. I was content.

In the spring of 2006, my principal asked me to leave my comfortable position in third grade to teach fourth grade. The writing scores were not what they should be in fourth grade, and she knew of my hard work and ongoing research in that area. I didn't want to go, but I agreed. My first year teaching fourth grade went well, and I had the privilege of teaching many of my previous third graders, which was a welcome treat. My class scored 90 percent on the state writing test, and I was pretty pleased. Our grade level as a whole, however, scored only 72 percent, and our principal was concerned. It was at this point she asked me to departmentalize. As you can see, my principal asks a lot of me, and I am proud that she does. So here begins my tale of challenges, commitment, perseverance, and the writer's notebook.

I have always had an interest in using a writer's notebook in my class. I remember creating my own stories and poetry as a little girl and proudly presenting them to my parents. My black-and-white composition book was always close at hand. I recall one time trying to write a story very similar to *Little House on the Prairie*. I adored that series and read the books over and over again. I changed the names and most of the events in my story, but one thing I kept from the original was Pa playing the fiddle. As my mother read my prized piece, she smiled and reminded me I shouldn't try to imitate other authors—I should be original. She suggested that I change my story. I hung my head and never completed my masterpiece. The irony is that, as a writing teacher, I am constantly telling my students that it's OK to borrow craft and structure from our favorite authors. Most of us even write with a style similar to that of the books we like the best. It's what many real writers do. Many real writers also keep a writer's notebook.

I had attempted to use the writer's notebook in my classrooms for years. I categorized and micromanaged those notebooks until they became mine, not something my students fell in love with, thought were useful, or felt were their own. When my students tried to use their notebooks, I admit I couldn't offer much guidance. I was also struggling with figuring out the purpose and curricular connection the notebook had to writing. Eventually I just pushed them to the side.

It was the summer before my first year as a fourth-grade teacher at my current school. I had taught many of the students the year before and wanted to make sure my writing lessons and ideas were not just repeats from third grade. This is when I really began to study the reasoning behind having a writer's notebook in the first place. I went back to the drawing board. I read every article and book I could get my hands on regarding not only how to use the writer's notebook but also how to be an efficient writing teacher. I let Donald Graves and Donald Murray guide my study and open up the world of the writer's workshop and the writing process. It was Lucy Calkins and Katy Wood Ray who taught me about inquiry and units of study. And I certainly can't forget how Vicki Spandel and Ruth Culham held my hand through the maze of this language we call the 6 Traits. I had studied these great writers before, but this time I studied with my eyes wide open and with purpose. I was ready for my new class year to begin.

I will never forget my excitement at introducing the writer's notebook to my students. I had all of my lessons ready to go. I decided we would use our notebooks for free writing, a time when my students could openly express themselves.

I started each day with a book. I didn't categorize or select my books based on any particular notebook connection; I was just determined to expose my students to good literature. After I read, we talked about the book, and then I asked my students to go and write whatever they wanted in their notebooks. Whatever they wanted. This was their free moment to explore their thoughts and life events. This was our routine for several weeks. Many students struggled with what to write in their notebooks. I told them, "Anything you want!" Then it came time to start planning a narrative story that we would later draft and publish. We put our notebooks away, and I pulled out the graphic organizers I like to use .We were on our way to writing success. I was still using prompts in my classroom at this time, so my students didn't get much self selection except in the notebooks, but we did not publish much that was in there. The notebooks were more like daily journals. The narratives were pretty good, so I decided it was time to begin writing expository essays.

Our state writing test is based on these two modes of writing, so it was important to make sure that these forms of writing were thoroughly covered. I gave my students a prompt for their essays, and they published those as well. By this time it was close to November, and I knew we needed to go back over narrative writing, and so the story continues until February when the state writing test was administered. What happened with our notebooks? Well, we returned to those after the test and used them in the same manner as we had at the beginning of the year. Now in defense of my teaching, my class did score high, with a 90 percent proficiency rate, so not all was lost, but, did I sense excitement and joy from my students? No, not really. Did I find myself focusing more on the state writing test than on my purpose for teaching writing? Yes. Did I lose sight of the foundations of a true writer's workshop? Yes, I did. And, most importantly, was I more concerned with the product rather than the process? Unfortunately I was. Why, after all that study, did I resort to my old teaching methods? Because I still felt like I was missing a connection with regards to the whole notebook thing. I went back to what I was used to; the old way was easier. I can't say it was a conscious decision, just a natural one. Teachers, like most, are creatures of habits and routines. This is the trap I fell into. Thank goodness I am a reflective teacher, one who is always thinking, always rethinking, and always trying to improve. I did not feel my entire year was a loss. After all, we had utilized our notebooks in a way that gave my students moments of freedom, even if briefly. But I knew I wanted more, and my students deserved more. I was determined to get it right.

Let me jump to the following year, the year I was asked to departmentalize. After 19 years of teaching, this is the one I will never forget. You see, I found the missing pieces to the puzzle that year. My students were filled with energy and excitement every time they wrote. I touched their lives, and they forever imprinted mine. I made a difference. I connected to the process, and my students followed me and let me guide them. Together, we were a community of writers. We practiced and became collectors and selectors, and took time to marinate before drafting. I rarely used prompts, so my students found their voices. Our fourth-grade state writing score rose from 72 percent the previous year to an astounding 94 percent. When my principal called me at three o'clock in the morning with the results (as I said, we are very close), I cried . . . literally dropped to my knees and cried. We had worked so hard, and my students had believed in me, and I had believed in them. If this book can help any teacher feel that moment, any student fall in love with and nurture the writing process and the notebook, then all the sleepless moments it took to write this, and the years it took to prepare and collect for it, have been worthwhile. Let me take you on my journey, step by step.

## Chapter One

# The Fundamentals of the Writing Workshop

"Children deserve to be explicitly taught the skills and strategies of effective writing, and the qualities of good writing."

—Lucy Calkins

## What Is a Writing Workshop?

If I were asked to give a formal definition of a writing workshop, I would define it this way:

- A sustained, daily writing on topics that are mostly self-chosen because students' comfort lies in what they know best.
- Writing for purposes and audiences that the writer values and understands. (See Author's Purpose on page 2.)
- Playing around with language and learning how to craft writing.
- Conferring with students and responding to their writing with explicit language.
- Celebrating what students have done well, and teaching them the next steps for moving forward.
- Modeling what real writers do to make a piece engaging for the reader.
- Guiding students through the writing process, always focusing on the process instead of the product. (See The Writing Process on page 2.)
- Publishing for real audiences.

In other words, the writing workshop invites students to do all the things a writer does.

## Author's Purpose

The writing workshop also holds to the belief that writing is for a purpose and for an audience. This purpose and the audience give the writing the "voice" that it needs. If my students are working on a persuasive piece of writing, then their purpose is to prove "why," and I should hear that theme reflected in the writing.

I like to give my students an "author's purpose" reference chart that helps them determine the intended audience and the purpose of the piece they are working on. (See Figure 1.1 below.) I have this same chart displayed in my room. The PIEES mnemonic device is easy for students to remember.

For each different author's purpose, the voice changes. Many teachers come speak to me after one of my county workshops, asking how to *show* students what "voice" means. My two suggestions:

1. Expose students to a variety of literature that represents each of the authors' purposes. The more students hear the differences between the purposes, the easier it will be for them to add voice to a piece of writing.
2. If teachers allow students the freedom to choose what topics to write about, the voice will be natural and the passion for the self-selected topic will be evident. Choice equals voice. Caring about a topic has a lot to do with how good the writing will be.

## The Writing Process

I feel it is necessary to elaborate a little further on the steps in the writing process. There are many variations to the writing process. The steps I teach my students seem a little less traditional than the standard prewrite, draft, revise, edit, publish,

**Figure 1.1**  Author's Purpose (PIEES mnemonic)

| | |
|---|---|
| **P**ersuade | **E**xplain |
| **I**nform | **S**how Emotion |
| **E**ntertain | |

and share. When Donald Murray, a Pulitzer Prize-winning journalist, teacher, and author identified the steps in the writing process, he clearly wanted writers to make the steps their own. He feared that even naming steps could create rigidity. He hoped it would not.

Over the past several years, the focus of writing instruction has shifted from product to process. There are numerous ways to model this multistep process. The most common model is the first one, shown in Figure 1.2 below. It was created by Donald Murray and involves five steps of the writing process. The models shown in Figures 1.3 and 1.4 consist of only three steps. The models shown in Figures 1.5 and 1.6 (page 4) are longer and involve more than five steps.

**Figure 1.2**   Donald Murray (1982)

| | |
|---|---|
| 1. Prewriting | 4. Editing |
| 2. Drafting | 5. Publishing |
| 3. Revising | |

**Figure 1.3**   Donald Graves (author/researcher, 1975)

| | |
|---|---|
| 1. Prewriting | 3. Postwriting |
| 2. Composing | |

**Figure 1.4**   James Britton (researcher, 1970)

| | |
|---|---|
| 1. Conception | 3. Production |
| 2. Incubation | |

**Figure 1.5**   Vicki Spandel (teacher, writer, developer of the 6 Trait model, 1984)

| | |
|---|---|
| 1. Life | 5. Revising |
| 2. Finding ideas | 6. Editing |
| 3. Drafting | 7. Publishing |
| 4. Sharing | 8. Assessing |

**Figure 1.6** Amy Ludwig (Teachers College Reading and Writing Project)

| | |
|---|---|
| 1. Finding a seed | 4. Revision |
| 2. Nurturing a seed | 5. Publishing |
| 3. Drafting | 6. Celebration |

The writing process is not completed in sequential order. Some steps are repeated within one journey to publication. To me, the worst mistake a writing teacher can make is to "corral" students together through the steps, hoping that the products will be completed at the same time. When teachers say they *use* the writing process, it probably means they are *describing* it. Unless teachers are *modeling* the steps, students are not fully grasping the process. The writing process we use in my classroom consists of 12 steps, shown in Figure 1.7, below.

There is no one process for writing, but I have found that the one I use in my classroom combines the important components needed for the journey to publication. It may seem intimidating to some teachers because of the number of steps, but in actuality, it has simplified my teaching of writing and given a clear focus for my students. Writing is not by nature a speedy activity but a reflective one. I want to make sure I allow my students the beauty of time to reflect, self-assess, and share with others. Donald H. Graves, a pioneer in education, says, "The best change occurs slowly and comes from teachers themselves. It takes longer but it lasts." The process that I have designed and that we use in my classroom provides these reflective moments, and the change I see in my students as writers is measurable in their attitudes, scores, and state mandated test results.

**Figure 1.7** My Classroom Writing Process

| | |
|---|---|
| 1. Practicing | 7. Revising |
| 2. Collecting | 8. Sharing* |
| 3. Selecting | 9. Editing |
| 4. Marinating | 10. Sharing* |
| 5. Drafting | 11. Publishing |
| 6. Sharing* | 12. Sharing* |

*A note about sharing. My students typically share two times during their journey through the process. Sharing appears more frequently in this list because I wanted to show you where it *could* occur.

# Why Establish a Writing Workshop?

I always like to answer this question with a simple, yet poignant story called "The Red Flower," shown in Figure 1.8 on page 6.

Teaching students how to write is hard. In my experience, students who are given choice and ownership in their writing will step up to meet the expectations of the teacher. The accountability is there because the teacher respected the thoughts and ideals of the student. It's as if by allowing choice and freedom of what to write, the teacher is saying, "I value you, and I respect the writing choices that you make." Teachers want students to care about their writing, and in a writing workshop, where students have a sense of ownership and personal investment as well as a safe environment to explore their writing potential, this caring is evident.

# Major Tools of the Writing Workshop

To set up a successful writing workshop, there are several major tools that need to be in place right off the bat.

- A writing environment
- A predictable schedule
- A writer's notebook
- Mini-lessons
- A supportive community of writers
- Student and teacher models
- Mentor texts
- Methods for conferencing
- Strategies for sharing
- Units of study

### A Writing Environment

I am a product of my environment. I write best in an area that is quiet and organized. If my environment is chaotic, I will more than likely not produce my best writing. I also want to be comfortable in order to do my best work. I have found that most students are not much different. Let's take a closer look at:

- A meeting spot
- Housing materials and tools
- Arrangement of desks
- Special writing spots

**Figure 1.8**  Why a Writing Workshop?

### The Red Flower

Justin was a little boy who loved to draw.

One day his teacher told the class they were going to draw a picture.

Justin was very excited. He thought of all the wonderful things he could draw:

A dinosaur, a ship on the ocean, or even his friend Chris.

The teacher said, "We are going to draw a flower."

Justin was disappointed. He thought for a moment and began to dream of the beautiful flower he could draw. Maybe he should draw a daisy or even a red dandelion.

The teacher said, "This is how you draw a flower. First, you make a yellow circle in the middle. Then, you add six red ovals around the circle. Finally, you draw one straight line down from the stem and add a green leaf on the side."

Justin felt disappointed but did as he was told.

Six months later, Justin moved across town and began at a new school.

Justin's new teacher was interesting. She wore long flowing dresses and large gold hoop earrings.

One day after lunch, the teacher announced, "Today we are going to draw a picture."

Justin waited patiently for instructions.

The teacher walked over to his desk and asked, "What is the matter Justin? All the other children are drawing."

Justin said, "But I don't know what to draw."

The teacher patted Justin on the back. "Draw whatever you like, Justin. The sky is the limit. Use your imagination."

Justin took out a piece of paper and his crayons.

First, he made a yellow circle in the middle. Then, he added six red ovals around the circle.

Finally, he drew one green straight line down for a stem and added a green leaf on the side.

—Author unknown

**A Meeting Area.** At the front of my room, I have a meeting area where my students and I gather every single day. I want to pull my students in close to me. It is in this area that the mini-lesson is taught. To create the meeting area, I simply purchased a bright and inviting area rug, and voilà! I ask my students to come prepared each day to our meeting area. They know that they need their writer's notebook and a pencil. I typically sit in the author's chair to introduce the lesson and read from the mentor text. Our author's chair is a simple hand-painted director's chair that is attractive and comfortable. This meeting area is also the place during independent writing where I work with students who need further assistance.

**Housing Materials and Tools.** A writer needs easy access to tools. There is nothing more frustrating than not being able to find something when you need it. I keep the following items handy and accessible for my students at all times. These items are stored in an area I call the Writing Center.

- A basket of blue pens for revising
- A basket of red pens for editing
- A large container of small, medium, and large sticky notes
- Dictionaries, laminated word lists, thesauri, and checklists
- Editing wheels
- Index cards for research
- Drafting folders
- A basket of eraserless pencils for drafting (I want my students to make mistakes.)
- A box filled with pink pearl erasers

**Arrangement of Desks.** I have found that clustering the classroom desks in groups makes conferencing easier and creates mini-communities within the classroom. When it is time to share pieces of writing, having these groups already set up and ready saves valuable time. I also have tables strategically placed throughout the room. My students do not have to write at their desks. Some enjoy using a clipboard and sprawling across the floor. Others like a secluded cubby area where papers can be spread out and evaluated. I want my students to have the mobility and freedom to figure out who they are and the conditions in which they work best as writers. Spreading out also helps with noise control.

**Special Writing Spots.** Professional writers have work spaces that they visit each day to write. I ask my students to do the same thing. A special writing spot is simply a self-selected writing spot where a student likes to work. I collect bean bags and large pillows to add a little comfort for those who choose to work on the floor. I also ask that my students select a spot that is "an arm's length away" from another student. This special writing spot is kept for several weeks, and sometimes all year, if the student chooses. After independent writing, I dismiss my students to their special writing spots. It is at these spots that I conference and work one on one. If I find that two or three students are having difficulty with the same skill, punctuating dialogue, for example, then I ask these students to leave their special spots and join me at the meeting area.

I like sharing real-life examples with my students as often as I can. At the beginning of the year, when students are selecting their special writing spots, I share the following examples of the special spots or work spaces of three famous writers:

1. Flannery O'Connor wrote in front of a blank wall to avoid any distractions.
2. Patricia Polacco begins each composition by sitting in one of her twelve rocking chairs at home.
3. Mem Fox begins each day with a clean and organized work area. She always uses a pencil first, and she must work in a place of solitude and silence.

By giving my students these examples, I continue to show them that, in our classroom, we live like writers.

## A Predictable Schedule

Writing workshop is a daily time set aside for students to write. Its time must be predictable. Students flourish with steadfast routines and understood expectations. Students need to know that they will write every day so that they can anticipate, plan, and find a writing rhythm. A writing workshop should be as predictable as a daily lunch schedule. My students know when lunch is, how to gather the necessary supplies (tray, milk, fork, straw, etc.), and the routine for punching a lunch card number into the monitoring system. My students also know the rules for carrying their tray and the predetermined seating arrangement. There is no confusion or question about what to do during lunch. Why? Because from day one, the routines and expectations were established.

If we hold true to this in a writing workshop, then our time is focused on teaching, and we, as teachers, know we must make the most of every minute. I am fortunate to have 60 minutes available in my schedule for writing workshop. I know there are many schools where only 30 to 45 minutes are allotted for writing each day. Make the most of it. Set those routines and hold firm to them. This will eliminate wasted educational time. With repetition comes the peace of knowing what to expect, and knowing what to expect leads to student independence. I know that if I were to walk out of my classroom to grab a cup of coffee, my students would know exactly how to carry on without me. I am not implying that I do this, but it is comforting to know that my students are in control of their learning. Lucy Calkins, Founding Director of the Teachers College Reading and Writing Project, has been quoted as saying, "A good writing teacher works herself out of a job."

**Timeline for a Typical Day in Writer's Workshop.** My writer's workshop is 60 minutes long. A good rule of thumb is that 50 percent of your students' time in writer's workshop is spent doing independent writing. The other 50 percent is used for mini-lessons, try-its, and sharing. (See Figure 1.9 below.) We gather at our meeting spot (a carpeted area at the front of the room by the whiteboard) at the beginning of every writer's workshop. Gathering like this creates unity and a sense of a writing community. Here is my breakdown of the time in writer's workshop:

1. The teacher and students gather at the meeting area. The students bring their notebooks with them to the meeting area. The teacher reads all or part of the mentor text, then introduces the mini-lesson, keeping it short and focused. Most of my mini-lessons are based on the mentor texts. **(15–20 minutes)**
2. The teacher repeats the specific craft or strategy from the mini-lesson. **(2 minutes)**

**Figure 1.9**  Instructional Time

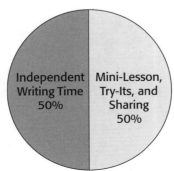

3. The teacher models the specific craft or strategy for the students on an anchor chart. This is called a "think aloud." **(5 minutes)**
4. The students "try-it" (the craft or strategy from the mini-lesson) in the **back** of the notebooks. **(3 minutes)**
5. Students turn and talk to an elbow partner about what they just did in their notebooks. Then a few are shared aloud. **(2 minutes)**
6. The teacher adds the sharing to the anchor chart. **(2 minutes)**
7. Now it is time for the students to leave the meeting area and go to their special spots for independent writing. During this time, I confer with my students. **(25 minutes)**
8. Students bring their notebooks back to the meeting area to share. **(5 minutes)**

These times are not set in stone but rather are a framework for making the most of your workshop time. If your workshop time is less than 60 minutes, then the best place to cut to your time is the mini-lesson. Try to make the mini-lesson as concise as possible, and if you need to, stretch the one lesson over the course of two days. Remember that actual writing time (independent writing) is the most valuable time. Donald H. Graves pressed this point when he said, "The more a writer writes, the more processes of choice and rehearsal occur." You can see that the notebook is used during the mini-lesson, again at independent writing time, and finally during sharing. The fundamentals of using a writer's notebook are covered in Chapter Three.

**Real Writers Have Routines.** I like to share with my students three examples of the routines of famous writers.

1. Stephen King keeps a strict routine each day. He starts each morning with a cup of tea and a vitamin. He sits down to work between 8:00 and 8:30 and doesn't stop working until he has at least 10 pages typed. He says that sometimes these 10 pages take a couple of hours, and sometimes they take all day long and into the night.
2. When John Grisham first began writing, he still had his day job as a lawyer. He woke each morning at 5:00 and headed to his office five minutes away. He claims that he had to be sitting at his desk with a cup of coffee and a yellow legal pad by 5:30. His goal was to write one page per day.
3. In describing her own routine, Toni Morrison reveals the importance of rituals to writers. Her own ritual involves making a cup of coffee and watching the light come into the day. Her

habit of rising early was first formed as the mother to three children, but after her children left home, she discovered a routine of her own that still includes early mornings. Morrison urges all writers to look at what time of day they are most productive and what type of surrounding is most conducive to their work to help form rituals that will promote creativity.

One of the best books I have found that shares snippets of information and advice from real writers is *The ABC's of Writing for Children*. The information in this book was compiled by Elizabeth Koehler-Pentacoff. In this book, writers talk about their craft, where ideas come from, and living the life of a writer. I find myself referring to it again and again when I am looking for sample "dos and don'ts" to share with my students.

## A Writer's Notebook

In my classroom, a standard black-and-white marbled composition book becomes a special place to store ideas and plan for pieces of writing. Ralph Fletcher, in his book *A Writer's Notebook*, delights my students every year with his personal examples of his own notebook entries. I always recommend that teachers add this delightful book to their personal collection of resources. In Chapter Three, I break down the purpose of the writer's notebook in our workshop and how my students and I make the most of every page.

The writer's notebook plays an integral part in each facet of our writing workshop. Here is a brief breakdown of when and how the notebook is used:

- At the beginning of the year, the notebook is a place to free-write and explore ideas.
- Students use the notebooks to practice skills they have learned during mini-lessons.
- Later on, the notebook becomes a safe place for students to collect their ideas.
- After careful selection, the notebook houses student planning for a piece of writing.
- The back of the notebook is a reference tool that students can use throughout the year.

## Mini-Lessons

A mini-lesson is a short piece of direct instruction focused on a single topic. In several of the chapters in this book, I cover the mini-lesson and curriculum thoroughly. I believe it is helpful to know that I categorize my mini-lessons the following ways:

- Procedures (rituals and routines)
- Writer's notebook
- Writing process
- Genre study

I would like to give you a breakdown of some sample lessons that go in each category. At the beginning of each year, I review the standards and objectives as well as core strategies and lessons that have proven successful in the past, and I begin to plug this information into the category it belongs best. I use this same guide for mini-lessons when I look closer at my long-range planning. This is by no means my entire list of mini-lessons I need to cover, but I believe it will give you a great place to start. If you use the 6 Traits in your classroom, and I do, I have included the moment in the process when I focus on a trait.

## PROCEDURES

Status of the class
6-inch voice
Knee-to-knee conference
Using and taking care of
    materials
Entering and leaving the room
Our daily schedule
Ways to ask for help
Record-keeping procedures

Independent writing guidelines
Using the Alphasmart to
    prepare drafts
Author Web sites
Rules for computer use
Self-evaluation of work
Procedures for sharing work
Places for peer conferences
Portfolios

### Writer's Notebook (WNB)

Launching the notebook
Customizing the notebook
The purpose of the WNB
Structure (front: freewrite/
    back: reference)
WNB expectations
Using the WNB during a read
    aloud
Artifacts for the WNB
Rubric for grading

Writing smorgasbord
WNB dig
Linking the WNB to
    independent writing
Sketching in the notebook
Daily pages
Saving writing you admire
Parts of the notebook
Living the writerly life

## PROCESS
### Collecting (TRAIT of IDEAS)

Heart map
Writing back
Webbing
Writers collect words
Listing
Column charts
Questioning potential ideas

ABC chart
Looking for details
Collecting dialogue
Adding action to dialogue
Draw-label-question
Attributes
Topic T-chart

### Selecting (TRAIT of VOICE)

Notebook dig
Narrowing down choices
Questioning

Sharing idea with a writing
  partner

### Marinating (TRAIT of ORGANIZATION)

Marinating vs. planning
Quick sketch
Web
Storm and sort
W5 + H1 (who, what, where,
  when, why, how)

BME (beginning, middle, end)
Timeline
Handy planner
3-2-1 planner
Topic tree
Roller coaster

### Drafting (TRAIT of ORGANIZATION)

The "down" draft
The "up" draft
Tools for drafting
Author's purpose
Emphasis on content rather
  than mechanics

Cutting and pasting
Organizing a draft
Placing an X on every other line
Working through writer's block
Rules of diligent drafting

### Revising (TRAITS of SENTENCE FLUENCY and WORD CHOICE)

Meaning of revision
Using a blue pen to revise
Adding/taking away
Brilliant beginnings
  • Beginning with a participial phrase
  • Beginning with a conjunction

- Beginning with a question
- Beginning with a preposition
- Beginning with a setting description

Excellent endings
- Ending with a question
- Ending with a feeling
- Wrap around or circular ending
- Ending with dialogue
- Ending with a lesson learned

Strong verbs
Similes
Idioms
Sensory details
Alliteration
Adding emotions
Show don't tell
Hover moment (hot spot in a narrative)
Juicy color words

### Editing (TRAIT of CONVENTIONS)

Lessons on spelling
- Using a red pen to edit
- Forming plurals by changing *y* to *i* and adding *-es*
- Portmanteau words
- Syllabication
- Words with silent *e*
- Forming plurals by changing the spelling
- Spelling demons

Lessons on grammar
- Complete sentences
- Subject and verb agreement
- Keeping pronouns consistent with point of view
- Verb tense agreement

Lessons on punctuation
- How to use periods
- How to use commas (list, pause, appositive)
- How to use question marks
- How to use ellipses
- How to use apostrophes for contractions
- How to use apostrophes for possession

Lessons on capital letters
- Using capitals at the beginning of sentences

- Using capitals for proper nouns
- Using capitals for abbreviations

## Sharing (TRAIT of VOICE)

Author's chair
Peer sharing
Why do we share?
How to respond as a listener

What I liked/why T-charts
Two stars/a wish T-chart
Wows/wonder T-chart
Using whisper phones

## Publishing (TRAIT of PRESENTATION)

Using different types of paper
Creating a title
Creating a table of contents
Writing "About the Author"
Publishing on the computer
Binding a book

Sending your writing to kids'
    magazines and contests
Illustrations
Selecting pieces for the
    portfolio

## GENRE STUDY

### Expository
- Types of expository writing (information, directions, opinions, persuasion)
- Recognizing a topic sentence
- Adding details to a topic
- Sticking close to a topic
- Speaking directly to the reader
- Using humor in expository essays
- Structure of the five-paragraph essay
- Selecting fascinating facts
- Putting voice in nonfiction
- Coming up with good questions for research
- Writing a caption for a picture
- Brainstorming an expository prompt
- Organizing multiple paragraphs
- Expository grabbers
- Crafting nonfiction endings
- Varying placement of the topic sentence

### Narrative
- Structure of a narrative (beginning, middle, end)
- Conflict makes stories interesting

- Using a storyboard to plan
- Building a powerful plot
- Using character feelings to guide purpose
- Creating a dramatic scene
- Describing a setting
- The inner life of a character
- Focusing on a slice of pie
- Time focus
- Surprising your reader
- Plot peak organizer
- Creating story problems and solutions
- Finding narrative ideas from personal experiences

**Keeping It Organized.**   After sitting down and brainstorming what I need to teach my students, listing objectives and mini-lessons, and placing them into one of the four categories (procedures, writer's notebook, process, and genre), I create a list for each category. Then I place each page into a plastic page protector and file these pages in a 2-inch binder. When I teach a lesson, I use a Sharpie to record the date in a box I draw beside each lesson on the list. At the end of the year, I simply wipe the plastic clean and reevaluate my lists. I typically add new lessons to the lists, and sometimes I remove some lessons or join two or more lessons together. This method helps me. You should use whatever method you are comfortable with.

## Building a Community of Writers

Each summer I sit down at my old wooden teacher's desk and reflect on what worked and what didn't. I keep my handy yellow legal pad and my reflection journal right by my side. The fact that I keep a reflection journal helps me remember the teaching moments that I hope to repeat and those I might want to forget. After over 20 years of teaching, this type of reflection is one thing I can definitely say has helped me grow.

I also reflect during the school year. Each afternoon I sit at my desk for 10 to 15 minutes and think back over my lesson for that day, the way the students reacted to the lesson, any problems I may have had, and so on. It's like my teaching diary. Sometimes I vent over an attitude displayed by a parent or a discipline decision that I might want to look at more closely. Typically, I reflect on my curriculum. When I decided that I wanted to become a teacher, I accepted the challenge that I would have to adapt constantly, continue to learn, and be brave enough to reflect on the good, the bad, and the not so great moments in my career.

Within my classroom, I always try to build a community of writers, so that the students are not afraid to take risks and leave each day feeling success as a writer. Most teachers remember writing as the dreaded subject that was filled with prompts, red pens, and silent classrooms. I want to make sure that my students experience something different than I had when I was in school. My classroom community isn't perfect and there are areas I am still working on, but my students love to write, they are good at it, and as I continue to reflect each day, I am becoming a better writing teacher—and I can't ask for more than that. The following quote that I read many years ago still hits home with me today: "Palm trees grow in Miami—not Cincinnati." Teachers must remember that it is all about creating a warm and inviting climate in which their students can thrive as writers.

## Student and Teacher Models

**Foundations.** I like structure, and my students do, too. It is comforting knowing what is coming next and being mentally and physically prepared for it. I start the year by telling stories. I share stories, and my students share stories. It is important that we get to know each other before jumping headfirst into the curriculum. I want my students to know me as a writer and each other as writers. So the first few days of school, we have a standard greeting, we gather on the carpeted spot I have salvaged as a meeting area, and we talk. Students need many opportunities to talk and to listen. James Britton, researcher and author, reinforced this point when he said, "Writing floats on a sea of talk."

There are so many good books out there about telling stories, and I share many of them during this time. Here is a small sample of these books:

- *Tell Me a Story, Mama*, Angela Johnson
- *The Stories Julian Tells*, Ann Cameron
- *Oliver Has Something to Say*, Pamela Edwards
- *Arthur Writes a Story*, Marc Brown
- *Tell Me a Silly Story*, Carl Reiner
- *Tell Me My Story, Mama*, Deb Lund
- *Tell Me a Story, Daddy*, Moira Kemp
- *Tell Me a Story*, Jonathan London
- *Why Mosquitoes Buzz in People's Ears*, Verna Aardema (A great book to use when introducing the tradition of oral story telling.)

During this introductory time, I like to have my students complete a writing inventory, which helps me know a little more about them as writers. The information is stored in a writing portfolio. Our portfolio system is covered more thoroughly in Chapter Eight, but basically it is a collection of student writing that is kept, shared, and reflected upon until the end of the year. I like to use basic manila folders for our portfolios. Figure 1.10 (page 19) is an example of the writing inventory I use. This inventory is a great tool for initial conferencing with students, pairing up students with like interests, and making sure that I incorporate those interests into my writing curriculum. If, while reading over the inventories, I find that I have four boys and two girls who play soccer, I want to keep that in the back of my mind when searching for books, poems, magazine articles, and so forth.

**Student/Teacher Samples.** I am a firm believer in using writing samples to teach my students. These are also referred to as "anchor papers." I have been collecting samples for the past seven years. I categorize these samples by genre and by score. For example, I have a binder labeled Personal Narratives. In this binder I have close to 100 sample papers. Each is categorized based on a score of 1.0 to 6.0. In addition to categorizing them by genre and score, I evaluate a strength and a weakness of each piece of writing based on the 6 Trait model. I simply write this information on a sticky note and attach it to the front to the sample. I am still a fan of the overhead projector, so I like to make transparencies of each model, and as I am teaching from it, I can use a wet erase marker to point out the important craft features of a particular piece. It is also important that I show my students samples of my own writing. First of all, the students love seeing what teachers write, and secondly, it promotes the idea that trust is necessary for building a community of writers. I want my students to see that I have tried, at least once, what I am asking them to do. Real writing takes courage and reflection. The whole "process" feels less intimidating to students when they see pieces of writing from their peers and from their teacher. When teachers expose themselves to the writing process, they understand the process better because they have been there. One final note on writing samples: it is very important to pull anchor papers (samples) that are clearly problematic or clearly strong.

## Mentor Texts

Mentor texts are pieces of literature that teachers can return to time and time again to show students possibilities for structure

**Figure 1.10**  Student Writing Inventory

Name:

Date:

 1. I like to write?    Yes    No    Sometimes

 2. I am a good writer?    Yes    No    Sometimes

 3. I think writing is important?    Yes    No    Sometimes

 4. I like to show my writing to others?    Yes    No    Sometimes

 5. I write a lot?    Yes    No    Sometimes

 6. Others can understand my writing?    Yes    No    Sometimes

 7. The things I write about are interesting?    Yes    No    Sometimes

 8. My best writing piece was _____

 9. I'm best at writing _____

10. My favorite time to write is _____

    _____

11. My favorite place to write is _____

12. My favorite thing to write about is _____

    _____

13. The last writing I did was _____

14. Something I would like to write about is _____

    _____

**Teacher's Notes**:

and craft. I love the books I refer to as mentor texts, and I know what they have to offer. I study the possibilities and record my findings. I am not reading like a reader, but rather like a writer. The first time I introduce a mentor text to my students I approach it like a read aloud, and then I put the words through a sieve and collect the teachable moments. If I want my students to know how to study books in this way, I must model for them daily. It is also important for students to be exposed to a variety of genres and have time to explore the texts for the beautiful language and techniques used by popular authors. Children's author Mem Fox says that students who are not exposed to good books (mentor texts) live in a "literary desert." I have provided an extensive list of mentor texts in the reference section. Chapter Two elaborates on how to find mentor texts and create a writing curriculum that is personalized for your classroom and the needs of your students.

## Conferencing

During independent writing time, the teacher has the opportunity to work individually with students who need specific help. When I confer with my students, I am a "floater." I do not ask them to leave their special writing spots; I go to them. This decreases the amount of movement so it does not distract other students. My conference is basically a deliberate act of listening: I research the piece of writing, I decide on one area I feel would benefit the writer, and I teach the student at a one-on-one level. If I find two or three students with similar needs, I pull them from their special writing spots and conduct a small group conference. I cover the foundations and management basics of conferencing in Chapter Nine, "Conferencing with Confidence."

## Strategies for Sharing

We share at the end of writing workshop each day. Sharing gives writers a chance to address real audiences. It is imperative that positive feedback from peers be provided. There are many different methods for share time:

- Whole class. At the end of each day, we take time to share among the whole group. I typically have time for five students to share per day. If, while conferencing, I find a student who has practiced the mini-lesson for that day, I make a point of asking that student to share first.

- Small group. During independent writing, small groups of students may gather to ask each other for help and advice on a piece of writing they are working on. I require that if a small group decides to meet that they use a "6-inch voice" in order not to disturb the others working independently.
- Partner. It is typically during the drafting, revising, or editing step of the writing process that my students share with partners. I always remind my students to keep in mind that we are "partners . . . never targets." It is also during partner sharing that T-charts are used for recording thoughts about another student's piece of writing. In Chapter Six, I have included samples of these charts.

I believe that sharing is one of the fundamentals of the writing workshop, yet it often seems to be left out because of a lack of time, especially when it comes to whole-group sharing. It doesn't take more than 5 or 10 minutes at the end of each writing workshop to fit in whole-group sharing. I find that with many students, their eagerness to share is an indicator of how they view themselves as writers. And as teachers continue to build the trust and confidence of students, even initially reluctant sharers become those waving their hands wildly to volunteer. In Chapter Six, "Drafting and Sharing," I go into detail about the processes and procedures of sharing in my classroom.

## *Units of Study*

A unit of study is a series of mini-lessons on a focused topic that are grouped together. A unit of study generally lasts three to six weeks. Not all units of study are genre specific. Some other possible units include:

- The writerly life
- Revison
- Conventions
- Author's craft
- Mentor text study

A unit of study in teaching writing allows for:

- Deep and sustained thinking about a particular genre or skill
- Time to focus on important issues about writing and learn about them with depth and rigor (depth, not coverage)

The goals of teaching writing within a unit of study are to:

- Provide opportunities for students to produce pieces of writing that are written under the influence of that study
- Allow students the opportunity to discuss the process involved in the study and link mentor texts to the study
- Invite students to show actual finished pieces of writing from the study and collect these pieces in a portfolio

## A Final Note

A writing workshop provides a simple and predictable structure for students. It enables the teacher to demonstrate what she wants students to learn. By establishing rituals and routines, and a safe environment where students can take risks, and by using mentor texts to teach students to read like writers, teachers are creating a community of writers filled with students who love to write.

*Chapter Two*

# Using Mentor Texts to Create Curriculum

"The writing you get out of your students can only be as good as the classroom literature that surrounds and sustains them."

—Ralph Fletcher

## Welcome to My Library: Creating a Curriculum

The goal of this chapter is to help you create your own curriculum with the help from a few of your friends. These "friends" are the books right there on your shelves. These are not just any books, but those books that we, as teachers, connect to and find ourselves reaching for every year and sometimes several times a year. These are called *mentor texts*. Mentor texts are some of the most important tools in a writing workshop. Mentor texts are picture books, poems, articles, and so forth that the teacher and the students love and connect with. Chapter book excerpts can also be excellent examples for students. Here are a few of my favorite chapter book excerpts:

**1.** *Old Yeller*, by Fred Gipson
It was a sort of raging yell he let out when he was in a fight to the finish. It was the same savage roaring and snarling and squawking that he'd done the day he fought the killer hogs off me. The sound of it chilled my blood. I stood, rooted to the ground thinking what it could be, what I ought to do.

I use this as an example of rising action and suspense. The strong verbs and auditory images stay with the reader.

**2.** *Charlotte's Web*, by E. B. White

"Where's Papa going with that ax?" said Fern to her mother as they were setting the table for breakfast. "Out to the hoghouse," replied Mrs. Arable. "Some pigs were born last night." "I don't see why he needs an ax," continued Fern, who was only eight.

This is a wonderful example to share with students about starting a story with dialogue and grabbing the reader's attention.

**3.** *Alan and Naomi*, by Myron Levi

"NAOMI!" he shouted. "NAOMI! . . ." The wind blew the words back around him like a tattered scarf. Then he threw himself down on the landing field, deep in the weeds. And he cried into the ground until the ground itself seemed to be crying, caking his lips with mud.

This is an excellent example of ending a story with emotion as well as "show don't tell." The use of the simile provides my students with a concrete craft example.

I am a collector of books. I love them. I love the way they smell, the illustrations, the meaning behind each word. My students often ask, "Ms. Morris, if you could write like anyone, who would it be?" I honestly answer, "For children's literature, I want to write like Patricia Polacco with a dash of Cynthia Rylant and a pinch of Eve Bunting. In my adult writing world, I want to create stories like James Patterson and swirl in some Stephen King and Ann Miller. In my professional writing world, I'd love to write as beautifully as Katy Wood Ray and then blend in my two favorites—Donald M. Murray and Donald Graves. And to top it off, I want to write as honestly as Natalie Goldberg and Laraine Herring while using my writing to inspire others. The sheer brilliance of these writers inspires me every day. Oh, there are plenty others, but who has all day to hear me ramble on about my favorites, right?" My students laugh and I can see their brains thinking, "Wow, we thought she might just name one author." They quickly learn that I am as layered as I hope their writing becomes.

Honestly, I am in awe of writers. I appreciate every word they provide me and every teaching moment that their books hold. Many people say that one sign of a good book is that you don't want to put it down. I look at it differently. For me, one sign of a good book is that I *must* put it down in order to reflect and take notes on the techniques the author used. So now let me ask you, "If you could write like one of your favorite children's authors, who would it be? Or rather who would they be?" Make a list right now. This is an important first step. After you have your list of authors, off to the side write down the books they have written that you love. Not like but *love*. This second step may take a little longer. I would like to focus primarily on picture books for this study because they are more often used as mentor texts.

Now the third step is to go gather those books and a nice yellow legal pad. You might want to grab a couple of good sharpened pencils so you can be ready to create curriculum.

## Here We Go

Pick up the first book in your pile and read it. You have read it numerous times before so don't read it like a reader, go deep and read it like a writer. Notice the craft, the creativity, and the moments that made you grab the book in the first place. Take the time to notice the creative punctuation or use of text.

Now that you've read this picture book, go back to page one and study, really study, the words and the techniques. Look at how the author started the story. Are there any visual descriptions? Did the author start with the setting, or a character description, or possibly a little of both? This rereading is important because this is exactly what we want to teach our students to do.

Next, I would like you to grab that pencil and yellow legal pad and sit down in a nice comfortable place. Write down what you noticed on the first page. Write down the first few sentences. That is your *Notice It*. Now think, what technique did the author use? This is your *Name It*. It really doesn't matter what you name it, so don't get hung up on worrying about the exact word choice. It's simply important that you try. It won't be wrong; it will be enlightening. As long as you are consistent with your language, your students will become familiar with how you name the strategies.

It is time to go to the next page and the next. Your job is to document your noticings, and name them. Once you have exhausted the book, go back and review the information. For teaching purposes, try out the techniques you noticed in the book. This will be your *Try It*. It's hard isn't it? Yes it is, but please stop and remember that we ask our students to do the same thing. We ask for them to try new strategies and apply them to their own drafts or in their writer's notebooks. Congratulations! You have just walked in the same path as your students. As I have often said at workshops, in professional development opportunities, and even in the classroom, "I, as a teacher, must try out, at least once, what it is I am asking my students to do." I can't possibly teach something I've never tried. Well, I guess I could attempt to teach a writing lesson, but just how well I taught it may be questionable.

It is important to note that these moments you discovered in the picture books you love become mini-lessons for each stage of the writing process. Is there anything in this study that you do not want your students to apply to their own writing? I think probably not. Aren't we often told that we need to use concrete examples to help students see what we want them to do? Well, we now have those concrete examples. And if you believe, as I do, that you must try, at least once, what you are asking your students to do, you have now done that as well. The *Apply It* step will come when you celebrate the moments your students put these techniques in their own writing. This will more than likely happen during drafting, revising, or editing.

In one of my favorite mentor texts, *Fly Away Home*, by Eve Bunting, I have 25 different moments of craft listed in my study. That equals 25 different mini-lessons right at my fingertips. That is a lot of curriculum, and it is a good curriculum. It comes straight from the experts. It doesn't get any better than that. I have a partial listing of this information a little further on in the chapter.

## There Is No Real Curriculum for Writing

Many times teachers complain that writing has no curriculum in the traditional sense that other subjects have. But it actually does, and you can find that curriculum by walking over to your bookshelves. But what about the year-long curriculum programs that tell you when to teach what and sometimes even what to say? Those simply aren't for me. I may not like the books on the booklists that are provided, yet the lessons require me to teach with them. And the scripted curriculum is not my natural voice. Another problem I find with some of these programs is that they are inflexible with time. I may need three days to cover the skill of adding strong verbs, but a particular program gives me only one. Good grief, that is stressful for me. I have nightmarish visions of me saying to my students, "Today we will cover strong verbs and . . . hang on . . . let me grab my script so I will know what to say next . . . and by the way, let's get it right the first time because we only get today to learn it."

Please don't think I want to banish all curriculum programs. On the contrary, these programs have a place in the classroom, and it is up to you to determine just where they fit. Many writing programs provide a good foundation for beginning teachers who, after feeling comfortable with the process, may decide to develop their own lessons and guidelines. I have found that by stepping away from programs and stepping into my own writing examples and mentor texts I feel comfortable with, I become more connected to the curriculum. This is one of the major steps that helped me build my confidence to teach writing.

I am the self-professed "Copy Queen." Well, that used to be me. I have many preprinted lessons all nice and categorized in binders that I never use. If my classroom caught on fire, it wouldn't be those I would save. I'd save my students' writer's notebooks and portfolios, and as many baskets of my favorite books as I could get my hands on. That is where the real curriculum is. The preprinted lessons could just stay where they are.

## So Many Books, So Little Time: A Specific Study

You can teach an entire year of writing with fewer than 20 books. Because my district requires that I cover the genres of expository and personal narrative, I could choose 10 of my favorite mentor texts for each genre. Then, of course, I'd want to keep a nice basket of poetry and magazines handy. That's it. Now, before I give the impression that you should only have 20 books and two little baskets of poetry and magazines, I am not. I have hundreds and hundreds of books because I am a collector of books. But, if this many possibilities intimidated me, I'd simplify by pulling my 20 favorite books, letting those guide me for awhile, and then slowly adding as I go. I haven't studied all of my books, only those that have so much teaching potential that I feel an urge to open them up to study and share.

So if you find yourself concerned with the notion of "so many books, so little time," narrow your possibilities a little. Start by picking those books that you would save if your classroom was on fire. Then, challenge yourself to fall in love with a couple more books each year.

Does this sound too simple? Try it, and I believe you will find that it makes sense. Teachers are swamped with life, students, curricular demands, parents, and testing. And that is just in the first hour of each day. So slow down, take a deep breath, and go study your books. In Figures 2.1 and 2.2 (page 28), I've provided a few

**Figure 2.1**   My Study of *Fly Away Home,* by Eve Bunting

| Personal narrative writing | |
|---|---|
| *Notice It* | *Name It* |
| My dad and I live in the airport. | Beginning with a setting and shock statement grabs reader's attention. |
| Mr. Slocum and Mr. Vail were caught last night. | Concrete examples: people's names |
| He and I wear blue jeans and blue T-shirts and blue jackets. | Listing with *and,* also the repetitive use of the color word *blue* |
| Everything in the airport is on the move—passengers, pilots, flight attendants, cleaners with their brooms | Listing with commas |

**Figure 2.2**   My Study of *Coming on Home Soon,* by Jacqueline Woodson

| Personal narrative writing | |
|---|---|
| *Notice It* | *Name It* |
| *Ada Ruth,* she said. *They're hiring a colored woman in Chicago since all the men are off fighting the war.* | Italics to show dialogue |
| I love you more than snow. (This phrase is repeated throughout the book) | A patterned repetition of words for emphasizing an emotion |
| *Thank you, Lord,* grandma whispers when he puts the letter with mama's beautiful cursive in her hand. | Shows the climax or the point in the story when events begin to change |
| Pages 13 and 14 have no text, only illustrations | Spacing to show a passing of time |

examples of my personal-narrative book studies for you to look at, and of course to use, if you happen to love these books too. Figures 2.3 (page 29) and 2.4 (page 30) show examples of my book studies for expository writing.

**Figure 2.3** My Study of *Welcome to the Greenhouse*, by Jane Yolen

| Expository writing | |
| --- | --- |
| *Notice It* | *Name It* |
| Welcome to the green house. Welcome to the hot house. Welcome to the land of the warm, wet days. | This beginning repeats the words "Welcome to the." This grabs the reader's attention while also describing the setting. |
| in the green house, in the dark green, light green, bright green, copper green, blue green, ever-new green house. | Varied uses of the word *green* give the description depth. This is a great example to show students the importance of juicy color words. |
| a flash of blue hummingbird, a splash of golden toad, a lunge of waking lizards, a plunge of silver fish, a slide of coral snake through leaves, a glide of butterflies through air | The use of strong verbs to specifically describe the movements of certain animals gives the reader lasting visual images. |
| *a-hoo, a-hoo, a-hoo* *crinch-crunch* *pick-buzz-hum-buzz* *chitter-chitter-rrrrr* *kre-ek, kre-ek, kre-ek* *sniff-sniff-sniff* | This entire book is filled with examples of onomatopoeia. I like my students to create a web of all these examples we find in the text. |

As you can see, just from the four books in Figures 2.1–2.4, I have 16 mini-lessons and examples that I can use to help my students learn the craft of writing. In actuality, when I studied these four books, I had a total of 75 mini-lessons. That many mini-lessons could keep me busy for a good portion of the year.

Just how many mini-lessons do I teach in one unit of study? Let me start by showing you a framework of mentor texts and mini-lessons that I use. I call this study "specific" because, while studying these books, I pulled direct text examples from the books. Then

**Figure 2.4**  My Study of *The Lorax*, by Dr. Seuss

| Expository writing | |
|---|---|
| *Notice It* | *Name It* |
| But those *trees!* Those *trees!* Those Truffula *trees!* | Using italics to emphasize words. |
| He was shortish. And oldish. And brownish. And mossy. And he spoke with a voice that was sharp-ish and bossy. | Short and choppy sentences add rhythm (sentence fluency). Also the repetitive use of *-ish* words to describe. |
| Then . . . Oh! Baby! Oh! How my business did grow! | An excellent example of voice. |
| The Lorax said nothing. Just gave me a glance . . . just gave me a very sad, sad backward glance | The use of ellipses to add rhythm to sentences. Also the repetitive use of a simple word like *sad* for emphasis. |

I named the specific craft using the language that writers use. I need these text examples to show my students how writers really use the techniques I am asking them to notice, name, try, and apply. Later in this chapter, I will show you how I take this specific study and create a more general reference list. I go from *specific* to *general*. Why do I do this? Simply for convenience. I may have four or five pages of specific study from one mentor text alone. I need to keep a running document that will allow me to cross-reference my mentor texts with what I need to teach. For example, if I have determined that my students need to add dialogue to their writing, I go to my general chart, look for the books I listed that have good examples of dialogue, and pull the concrete examples from my studies of those books. Let's take a look at the general list of books (mentor texts) and craft (mini-lesson) that I use to guide, create, and teach my writing curriculum.

## Going from Specific Craft to General Craft

I like starting the year with a unit of study on writing a personal narrative. I gather some mentor texts and my general list of how I can use these books. In my pile of books, I have the following titles:

- *Brave Irene*
- *The Relatives Came*

- *Night in the Country*
- *An Angel for Solomon Singer*
- *Fly Away Home*
- *The Old Woman Who Named Things*
- *Owl Moon*
- *Thunder Cake*
- *The Harmonica*
- *The Great Fuzz Frenzy*
- *Hello Ocean*

At this point I brainstorm what I need to teach my students in this first unit of study on personal narratives. I look back at last year's lesson plans, and I brainstorm some new territory that I would like to teach. I understand that this planning is a framework because my students aren't here yet, and they are the breathing link to my curriculum. I will need to assess their writing needs before I finalize the long-range plans that I am making. But after 21 years of teaching, I have a fairly good idea of where to start.

I list the mini-lessons that I may start with—then I reach for my general list of mentor texts and mini-lessons. I pay close attention to the titles in the stack of books I just gathered. Figure 2.5 (page 32) shows you how I have documented what each mentor text has to offer.

My next step is to get specific. I need to pull concrete examples from the texts to serve as examples for my students. I used **boldface** type in Figure 2.5 to show you my decisions. This process resulted in the following strategies being taught:

- Beginnings
- Endings
- Strong verbs
- Similes
- Dialogue

## How Many Mini-Lessons Per Unit of Study?

I typically begin each unit of study planning on introducing four or five possible strategies. This number could change depending on time, student understanding, and a multitude of other reasons. Again, this planning is a framework. I may use this curriculum I have just designed when my students are drafting, revising, editing, or even publishing. Here are my justifications for why

**Figure 2.5** Craft from Mentor Texts

| Mentor Text | Mini-Lesson |
|---|---|
| *Brave Irene* | **Strong verbs**, person vs. nature theme, **dialogue** |
| *The Relatives Came* | **Beginnings: a setting, Endings: circular**, elapsed time |
| *Night in the Country* | Varying sentence lengths, personification, listing with commas |
| *An Angel for Solomon Singer* | **Beginnings: character/setting/ emotional tug, simile for sound**, elapsed time, **simile for sight** |
| *Fly Away Home* | **Beginnings: grabs reader, Endings: memory**, listing with commas, using italics to stress words |
| *The Old Woman Who Named Things* | Conversing with the reader, **dialogue**, setting apart names with quotations |
| *Owl Moon* | Metaphors, **simile for sound and hearing**, crafting a title, time focus |
| *Thunder Cake* | Beginnings: setting and mood, counting up, time focus |
| *The Harmonica* | **Beginnings: memory**, alliteration, varying sentence lengths, **simile for touch, sound, and status** |
| *The Great Fuzz Frenzy* | **Beginnings: problem, endings: circular, tagged dialogue**, alliteration, **strong verbs** |
| *Hello Ocean* | Sensory details |

and how I chose the five strategies I planned to start the personal-narrative unit with:

- I want my students to know several different options for **beginning** and **ending** their stories, so there are two.
- I know that **strong verbs** add much with regards to pace and visualization for the reader, so I want to teach them about strong verbs. That makes three mini-lessons.

- I believe that similes are crucial for providing the reader with a visual comparison. If a writer tells me the dog "is as large as an elephant," I can picture just how big that dog is. So that makes four mini-lessons so far.
- Dialogue is important to a piece of writing. It helps the reader connect to a character, it can add action to the critical part of a story, and it is effective when used to begin or end a piece of writing. I feel comfortable adding this strategy as my fifth mini-lesson.

I could keep going, but do I really need to? I feel comfortable with depth, not coverage. I can teach fewer mini-lessons, but spend a little more time on them or show more examples from mentor texts, and my students would have more opportunity to apply these mini-lessons to their own writing. That is what we want.

## Let's Go Back to Specific

I now have a goal of instruction in mind. It's now time for me to pull out my sheets of specific study and find concrete examples I need to use with my mini-lessons. Let's go to Figure 2.6 and take another look at my specific study of the book *Fly Away Home*, by Eve Bunting.

Because I know this book has good examples to show my students of how to begin and end a story, I can have this information at

**Figure 2.6**  My Study of *Fly Away Home*, by Eve Bunting

| Personal narrative writing | |
|---|---|
| *Notice It* | *Name It* |
| My dad and I live in the airport. | Beginning with a setting and shock statement grabs reader's attention. |
| Mr. Slocum and Mr. Vail were caught last night. | Concrete examples: people's names |
| He and I wear blue jeans and blue T-shirts and blue jackets. | Listing with *and*, also the repetitive use of the color word blue |
| Everything in the airport is on the move—passengers, pilots, flight attendants, cleaners with their brooms | Listing with commas |

my fingertips. I don't have to search through the book to figure out what I want to teach. That searching came with my specific study and was reviewed when I created my general list. And as for the other vital examples of text from *Fly Away Home*, I will use them at a later date. For example, when I see that my students need a lesson on how to list a set of items in their writing, I know this book shows two ways for them to do just that (with commas and with the word *and*). No moment of study is lost.

## Finding Time for the Lessons

Frequently I am asked how I fit a mini-lesson into the desired time frame of 15 to 20 minutes. (Recall that in Chapter One, I broke down my writer's workshop daily schedule and my mini-lessons range from 15 to 20 minutes a day.) For starters, I keep a pretty watchful eye on the clock, and I know that if an additional day of instruction is needed, I have the flexibility to use it. I also rarely read the entire mentor text when I am pulling specific craft; I only show examples from the books I am using to guide my lessons. That is where the specific study comes in handy: I have this information already at my fingertips. I reserve the first month or so of school for reading many mentor texts in preparation for revisiting them at a later date. Do not think that I never read a mentor text in its entirety because there are times I do. But if I have four or five examples of dialogue from different mentor texts I have studied, I simply show those dialogue examples I have found. There is no reason to read the entire book for that particular lesson.

Let me show you an example from the beginning of this process. If I want my students to beef up the beginnings of their drafts, I refer back to my study notes (the general list) and gather up the books that I know have strong beginnings. A few titles I may choose to use for this lesson are in Figure 2.7 (page 35).

Then I pull my specific study charts where I have concrete examples of each beginning documented. The single chart on page 35 shows five different ways to start a story. I could take two days to teach this revising skill to my students. I want to give them time to examine the examples and try out the different ways on their own stories, and, finally, I want to allow enough them enough time to share and select the one way that they feel best suits their personal narrative. That constitutes a full two days in my class. Remember,

**Figure 2.7** Sample Chart of Beginnings

These books begin with a . . .

- *Fly Away Home*: setting/shock statement
- *An Angel for Solomon Singer*: character/setting/emotion
- *Thunder Cake*: setting and mood
- *The Harmonica*: a memory
- *The Great Fuzz Frenzy*: a problem

I hold true to the principle that 50 percent of writer's workshop is spent in independent writing, so I need the mini-lessons concise and full of purpose.

## A Few Final Thoughts About Curriculum

My goal with this chapter is to let teachers see that they can and should be in charge of a subject that some educators feel has no real curriculum. The curriculum lies in the baskets on our bookshelves. It is at our fingertips and within reach of the students we teach.

The more you model and show your students how and why you have studied these particular books you are now calling mentor texts, the more they will begin to study as well. When my students studied books they loved, their insight in noticing and naming became more and more apparent as the opportunities were provided for them to read like a writer. After a couple of days, we would share these studies and learn from each other. We made anchor charts, discussed writings, and formed small study groups. It's really a beautiful thing to pull a chair up to a group of students and simply say, "Hey, do you mind if I study with this group for a little bit?" You will see them push their notebooks and pencils aside to make room for not just a teacher but, more importantly, a partner in this thing called writing.

## Student Samples of Study

When I ask my students to study mentor texts, I like to add the phrase "What I Liked" to the "Notice It" part of the chart. And I add the word "Why" to the section labeled "Name It." It seems to simplify the difficult task of identifying moments of craft and allows the students ownership in their selections. (See Figure 2.8 on page 37.) As the year progresses and the students become more comfortable with mentor text study, some continue to add the additional verbiage and some don't. It is up to them.

## Student Sample

The sample in Figure 2.9 (page 38) shows how one student was able to pull examples of craft from a mentor text, explain in his own words why he liked this example, and try to use the author's strategy in an example of his own.

**Figure 2.8** Study Chart

Book Title: _____

Author: _____ Genre: _____

| Notice It—<br>What I Liked | Name It—Why | Try It |
|---|---|---|
| | | |
| | | |
| | | |
| | | |

**Figure 2.9** Student Sample of Gathering Craft

(Note that the student's errors have been retained for authenticity.)

| What I liked | Why | Try it |
|---|---|---|
| She had a voice like slow thunder and sweet rain. | Uses a simile (like slow thunder and sweet rain) | She ran as fast as my . . . . Cheetah trying that to run toward its prey. |
| The three of us echanged looks. We wanted to get her that hat more than anything in the world. | In the first sentences I already new why they were exchanging looks It puts some suspence in there | We took a light glance at each other. We wanted to get that arête more than anything in the world. |
| Elua would always stop and look in the window at the wonderful hats. Then she'd sigh and walk on. | You already know that she wants one of the hats in the store. Strong adjective wonderful Scentence fluency | I would always stare at the blue and orange bass guitar. Then I checked my wallet and walk on. |
| Says slow thunder and sweet rain three times. | Reminds you of what you heared before | Beginning I'd smile when I was sad. Middle I'd smile when I was sad. End I'd smile when I was sad. |

*Chapter Three*

# Practicing in the Writer's Notebook

My Notebook

My writer's notebook to me is a forest. A forest of magic and wonder . . . a forest of ideas. Each little one is a seed you must nurture. You have to let the seed grow in its own special way because when it finishes growing, you will have a miracle. Your miracle will make more miracles, and with that, you will have an endless forest of ideas. Ideas that make up a life that you will cherish and pass on for an eternity. My writer's notebook is my everlasting treasure.

—Alex T.
10 years old
2008–2009 language arts class

## What Is the Purpose of the Writer's Notebook?

It is important to understand that the writer's notebook gives students a place to live like writers. It is equivalent to an artist's sketchbook or a musician's jam session. This is where students get into the habit of putting thoughts into words. It is a place to collect topics and practice mini-lessons. It also serves as a valuable reference tool, directly tied to a curriculum, which will be used again and again.

A writer's notebook stores ideas, thoughts, lists, wonders, artifacts, and passages from favorite books. I could go on and on. There really isn't much that can't go in the notebook, as long as it serves a purpose for writing. In my classroom, we have called them the following:

- Butterfly nets: Award-winning author Joanne Ryder says, "Ideas are like butterflies; you have to catch them quickly or they will escape and you may lose them."
- Seed packets: Writer and educational consultant Ralph Fletcher often refers to ideas as "seeds" just waiting to

germinate into a story. I enjoy reading Eric Carle's delightful book *The Tiny Seed* to help students see the analogy between seeds and ideas.

- Incubators: A writer's notebook is a holding tank for ideas until the journey to publication begins.
- Workbenches: A writer's notebook is also a place to store all the "tools" and ideas you need for writing a story.

It really doesn't matter what analogy you use, or whether you use one at all. The notebook is simply a very personal tool in which students pluck the specialness out of life and preserve it until they are ready to begin a piece of writing. The notebooks also maximize my writing lessons. My students have a handy resource right at their fingertips where reference charts are glued, pieces of writing are planned, and seed ideas are recorded.

## Make the Most of Every Page

There are approximately two hundred pages in a standard composition notebook. So how do we put them all to good use? Well, to answer that I need to remind you that writing notebooks are really two notebooks in one. The front of the notebook is preserved for practicing writing. The back of the notebook is used for collecting, reference charts, marinating, and mini-lesson "try-its." I will explain the back of the notebook in greater detail in the following chapters. I call the first step of the writing process that we use in my classroom "the practicing step." (The writing process is discussed in detail in Chapter One.) This practice happens during our independent writing time. It is the **front** of the notebook that my students go to every day during independent writing time.

## Possible Charts for the Notebook

As I said earlier, the front of the notebook serves as the spot for freewriting. I have many core charts that I like to give my students to help them generate ideas and make them feel comfortable with writing what is on their minds. Here is a list of the charts I provide for my students for the front of the notebook:

- Writing smorgasbord
- Proofreader's marks

- Narrative and expository prompt list
- Independent writing guidelines
- Writing notebook expectations
- Grading rubric

The charts in the back of the notebook are centered on the mini-lesson for the day. These charts enhance the mini-lessons. What I love about the back of the notebook being used as a reference section is that so much valuable information is right at the fingertips of my students. Here is a list of charts I provide for my students:

- Strong verb word list
- Onomatopoeia word list
- Simile and metaphor examples
- Awesome adjectives word list
- Juicy color word chart
- List of transitional phrases
- Parts of a friendly letter
- Sensory words list
- Sight word spell-check list
- Explanation of poetic devices
- Synonyms for *said*
- Literature examples of brilliant beginnings
- Literature examples of excellent endings

## Tabbing Important Pages

After a while, the notebooks become filled with entries and charts. It can be hard to locate where everything is. A few years ago, while watching my students flip through their notebooks in search of a particular reference chart, I announced, "OK, we are no longer going to be *flippers*, but rather *tabbers*!" I admit they all looked at me rather strangely. But by the time we had tabbed important pages, they appreciated my idea.

To tab a page we simply use small sticky notes. The name of the page being tabbed is written on the note and stuck to that page with just the title showing. If a student has a special entry in the front of their notebook that he wants to tab, that is fine too. These are their notebooks, and I want them to be comfortable personalizing and creating a true treasure that they will keep and duplicate for years and years.

**Figure 3.1**  Decorating Letter

Dear Parents,

We need your help! On _____, we are going to deco-
rate our writer's notebooks!! We are very excited. I talked to my students
today, and we brainstormed some items that we could use to personal-
ize the front of the notebooks. Here is our list:

1. pictures
2. ribbons (field-day type)
3. stickers
4. awards
5. magazine clippings
6. artifacts: tickets to a concert, movie, play, etc.

Please know that these items will be cut and pasted to the front of the
notebooks, so keep that in mind when collecting. We don't want anyone left out, so make sure your child is prepared for _____'s
decorating session.

Also, I need a couple of volunteers to cover our notebooks with clear
tape to help preserve all of our hard work. If you can help on that day,
please write me a note or send me an email.

Thank you,

_____

## Decorating the Notebooks

While I am on the subject of personalizing the writer's notebooks,
let me explain our procedure for decorating them. The first week of
school, I send home a letter to parents asking for their help in collecting pictures, ribbons, stickers, etc. that their child can use to decorate
the front of the notebook. (See Figure 3.1 above for a sample letter.)
This is always such an exciting day. The students take great pride in
making their notebook special and attractive. I like to use wide, clear
tape to preserve the pictures on the cover. I have tried contact paper
as well, but the tape works better for me.

## Guidelines But Not Boundaries

Each notebook entry is dated, and each page is numbered. I do not
control what my students write in the front of the notebook. That is

not to say I do not have expectations of meaningful writing. I just allow my students the freedom to select the form, shape, and topic of their daily writing. My students have a clear understanding of my expectations because at the beginning of the year we discuss the importance of living like a writer, how it is a solitary world, and how the chance to join writing groups and share when the hard work is finished is a reward in itself. It is my philosophy that whatever we are doing during writer's workshop should make us better writers. I do not believe that not writing is going to achieve this. You learn to write by writing, just like you learn to swim by swimming. When I was first learning to swim, I had a coach who taught me some "tricks of the trade," but ultimately it was through practice and trial and error that I became a proficient swimmer. This holds true for writers. So writing in the the front of the notebook serves as our practice and trial and error.

## "I Have Nothing to Write About!"

I know this question is going to come up: "What if a student complains he has nothing to write about?" It is a good idea to create an anchor chart of writing possibilities. We like to call this our writing smorgasbord. One year my students decided the "writing buffet" was a catchy title, so that's what we called it. I post this chart in an area of my room where students can see it and add to it as the need arises. On page 44, Figure 3.2 provides a sample of our anchor chart.

Many of these suggestions are broad, and that is fine. We want students to have room to explore. The last thing we want is for the notebook to feel like prompt writing.

## Teachers Must Keep Notebooks

It is important for me to start each year showing my students my notebook. I actually have many. My notebooks are filled with articles, photographs, and writings. One of my notebooks has a snippet of hair in a plastic baggie that is the result of my five year old trying to be a beautician. My students love the story behind that artifact. I have pictures of Labrador retrievers I rescued while I was living in Georgia. I always get choked up when I share some of these rescue stories with my students. Some of my writing I have sent off to be published, and some I simply save. All of it is important to me.

**Figure 3.2**  Writing Smorgasbord

| | |
|---|---|
| You might try to write about: | |
| • A collection of interesting words | • Lists of rhyming words |
| • Family stories | • Short stories |
| • Lists of likes and dislikes | • Commercials |
| • Quick sketches and captions | • Family traditions |
| • Close observations about the world | • Moments you were scared |
| • Quotes | • Character ideas |
| • Poems or songs | • Research |
| • Nursery rhymes | • Feelings or emotions |
| • Letters of complaint | • Fierce wonderings |
| • Book and movie reviews | • Snatches of talk |
| | • Stimulating conversations |

I keep a writer's notebook for two reasons: 1) because I am a writer, and 2) because I ask my students to keep one. If we expect our students to value the use of the writer's notebook we must walk the path with them. Teachers must also write. It is important that we try what it is we are asking our students to do. How can we teach and understand something we've never attempted?

For a while, I pondered what my students should write in their notebooks, and then I began to write in one myself and it all began to make sense. It is naive to assume that all we have to say to our students is "Write whatever you want in your notebooks," and they will. Remember, I tried that, and the results weren't that great. I found that a little more guidance is needed at first.

At the beginning of each year, I like to introduce the notebook with several core lessons that are centered on familiar picture books (mentor texts). I no longer randomly pull books off the shelf but study my books and discover what teaching possibilities they offer. At the end of this chapter, I provide you with ten of the lessons I created that helped my students be successful. I use these lessons the first ten days of notebook practice. These lessons were designed to slowly introduce the concepts of keeping and practicing in a writer's notebook, and how, if allowed, it will keep you. The last thing I want is for my students to go their special writing spots for independent writing time and not have a clear picture of what to do. The anchor chart, mentioned earlier, paired with thoughtful lessons, keeps expectations clear and excuses for not writing at a minimum.

## When Do We Use the Writer's Notebook?

This question may seem like an easy one but it was one I struggled with. Remember I was the teacher who, at first, used the notebook only the first two weeks of school and then again after the state writing test. Now our notebooks are used almost daily throughout the entire school year. If you refer back to the Timeline for a Typical Day in the Writing Workshop (page 9), you will find that use of the writer's notebook is evident in the following areas:

- Mini-lessons
- "Try-it" moments
- Independent writing time
- Sharing time

The writer's notebook is a critical tool in the writing workshop.

## Using the Notebook During Independent Writing

It is recommended that 50 percent of the writing workshop is spent in independent writing time. Students must have time to practice their writing, and this is the time to do it. The writer's notebook is used to collect and salvage this practice and provide conferencing opportunities. Let me offer you a chart (Figure 3.3, page 46) that I like my students to glue on the inside front cover of their notebooks. It gives them a framework of my expectations during independent writing time.

## Notebook Expectations

It is also important for students to know a teacher's expectations regarding the notebook. At the beginning of the year, when routines and guidelines are being formed, I like to provide my students with a chart of notebook expectations. (See Figure 3.4, page 46, for an example.) As a class, we discuss and elaborae on this chart, and then students glue it to the inside back cover. I want my students to have this type of information at their fingertips. This is important because if students tell me they aren't sure what to write in their notebooks, I can gently have them revisit the writing smorgasbord chart, the independent writing guidelines, and the notebook expectations. When you have provided your students with this much valuable information, it is hard for them to get too confused.

**Figure 3.3**  Independent Writing Guidelines

During independent writing I am . . .
1. Generating ideas and topics
2. Dating every entry and numbering each page
3. Practicing the daily mini-lesson strategy
4. Researching and collecting informaiton on topics that interest me
5. Sharing my writing entries with other students
6. Looking through picture books for ideas and craft
7. Sketching out a plan using words and pictures
8. Conducting interviews with other students
9. Drawing, labeling, adding captions
10. Reflecting on my life and experiences
11. Observing my surroundings for sensory details and potential writing possibilities
12. Referring back to the writing smorgasbord anchor chart for writing ideas

**Figure 3.4**  Notebook Expectations

1. Write daily in the front of your notebook. This is your chance to freewrite and explore. Feel free to refer to our writing smorgasbord anchor chart if you need writing suggestions.
2. Find topics for your notebook from your daily life, from reading, from observations, and from curiosity.
3. Try strategies from the mini-lesson in the back of your notebook, and then continue with your work for the day in the front of your notebook.
4. Fold over any entry that is too personal to share. It is a policy in our classroom to value everyone's privacy.
5. Respect the integrity of your notebook by taking care of it.
6. Practice what you know about conventional spelling and grammar. Entries must be legible.
7. Do not skip pages.
8. All drawings should have writing with them.
9. Number each page, and date each entry.
10. Make sure there is evidence of what you're learning in your notebook.

# Mentor Texts for Getting Started in the Notebook

Here is a list of books for practicing in the writer's notebook:

1. *Max's Words*, by Kate Banks
2. *Nothing Ever Happens on 90th Street*, by Roni Schotter
3. *The Boy Who Loved Words*, by Roni Schotter
4. *You Have to Write*, by Janet S. Wong
5. *Amelia's Notebook*, by Marissa Moss
6. *Amelia's Family Ties*, by Marissa Moss
7. *What If . . .* , by Regina J. Williams
8. *Pancakes for Breakfast*, by Tomie DePaola
9. *If You Were a Writer*, by Joan Lowry Nixon
10. *Arthur Writes a Story*, by Marc Brown
11. *The Picture That Mom Drew*, by Kathy Mallat
12. *The Stories Julian Tells*, by Ann Cameron
13. *Treasure of the Heart*, by Alice Ann Miller
14. *Voices in the Park*, by Anthony Browne
15. *Twilight Comes Twice*, by Ralph Fletcher
16. *I'm in Charge of Celebrations*, by Byrd Baylor
17. *Diary of a Worm*, by Doreen Cronin
18. *Show Don't Tell*, by Josephine Nobisso
19. *Read Me a Story*, by Rosemary Wells
20. *How a Book Is Made*, by Aliki

# Lessons for Practicing in the Writer's Notebook

## Book: *What If . . .* , by Regina J. Williams

### Day One

Strategy: Practicing in the notebook. Writers write using imagination.

What to do (1–7 is the mini-lesson):

1. Gather students at the meeting area with their writer's notebooks.
2. On large chart paper, create an anchor chart titled "What If . . ." The teacher explains the purpose of this strategy (to generate ideas for writing).
3. Read the book. Discuss genre, the author's purpose, time focus, connections, and information about the author's life.

4. Teacher adds his or her thoughts and ideas to the anchor chart (Think Aloud).
5. Students create a list in the **back** of their notebooks to resemble the anchor chart.
6. Students add to the list they have created. I am hoping the mentor text has helped generate some ideas for the list.
7. A couple of students share from their notebooks, and the teacher adds to the anchor chart.
8. Students write independently in the **front** of their notebooks for a set amount of time.
9. Students share. If a student has taken an idea from the day's mini-lesson and elaborated further on it, I let that student share first to help emphasize the strategy.

I also like to give my students a copy of Shel Silverstein's poem "Whatif" to glue in their notebooks. A student sample of this lesson is shown in Figure 3.5 (page 49).

## Book: *Yours Truly, Goldilocks*, by Alma Flor Ada

### Day Two

Strategy: Practicing in the notebook. Writers write letters.

What to do (1–7 is the mini-lesson):

1. Gather students at their meeting area with their writer's notebooks.
2. On large chart paper, create an anchor chart titled "Reasons to Write Letters." The teacher explains the purpose of this strategy (to generate ideas for writing).
3. Read the book. Discuss genre, the author's purpose, time focus, connections, and information about the author's life.
4. Teacher adds his or her thoughts and ideas to the anchor chart (Think Aloud).
5. Students create a list in the **back** of their notebooks to resemble the anchor chart.
6. Students add to the list they have created. I am hoping the mentor text has helped generate some ideas for their list.
7. A couple of students share from their notebooks, and the teacher adds to the anchor chart.
8. Students write independently in the **front** of their notebooks for a set amount of time.

**Figure 3.5** Student Sample for Day One Lesson

(Note that the student's errors have been retained for authenticity.)

|  | What If . . . |
|---|---|
|  | Clouds could come to life ✔ |
|  | Scary monters went away |
|  | Pine tree flowers ✔ |
|  | It snowed snowflake peprment ice-cream ✔ |
|  | I had wings and fly ✔ |
|  | Candy garden |
|  | Boxing kangaroo ✔ |
|  | Dogwood tree ✔ |
|  |  |
|  | Sudenly I woke up and though about the what ifs. What if clouds came alive and they let me soar up in the air. What if I had my very own boxing kangaroo as a bodyguard. What if I had a money tree that grew me money every day. What if it snowed and rained ice-cream and sweets. What if I had my own dogwood tree in my backyard that grew me pupys every day. What if I had a candy garden that grew me candy for every holday. What If . . . What If . . . My what ifs slowly drifted away as I fell into a deep sleep. |

9. Students share. If a student has taken an idea from the day's mini-lesson and elaborated further on it, I let that student share first to help emphasize the strategy.

## Poem: "The Turkey Shot Out Of the Oven," by Jack Prelutsky

### Day Three
Strategy: Practicing in the notebook. Writers write poems.
What to do (1–7 is the mini-lesson):

1. Gather students at the meeting area with their writer's notebooks.
2. On large chart paper, create an anchor chart titled "What We Know About Poetry." The teacher explains the purpose of this strategy (to generate ideas for writing).
3. Read the poem. Discuss genre, the author's purpose, time focus, connections, and information about the author's life.
4. Teacher adds his or her thoughts to the anchor chart (Think Aloud).
5. Students create a list in the **back** of their notebooks to resemble the anchor chart.
6. Students add to the list they have created. I am hoping the mentor text has helped generate some ideas for their list.
7. A couple of students share from their notebooks, and the teacher adds to the anchor chart.
8. Students write independently in the **front** of their notebooks for a set amount of time.
9. Students share. If a student has taken an idea from the day's mini-lesson and elaborated further on it, I let that student share first to help emphasize the strategy.

## Book: *Cinderhazel*, by Deborah Nourse Lattimore

### Day Four
Strategy: Practicing in the notebook. Writers write fairy tales.
What to do (1–7 is the mini-lesson):

1. Gather students at the meeting area with their writer's notebooks.
2. On large chart paper, create an anchor chart titled "Fairy Tale Facts." The teacher explains the purpose of this strategy (to generate ideas for writing).
3. Read the book. Discuss genre, the author's purpose, time focus, connections, and information about the author's life.

4. Teacher adds his or her thoughts and ideas to the anchor chart (Think Aloud).
5. Students create a list in the **back** of their notebooks to resemble the anchor chart.
6. Students add to the list they have created. I am hoping the mentor text has helped generate some ideas for their list.
7. A couple of students share from their notebooks, and the teacher adds to the anchor chart.
8. Students write independently in the **front** of their notebooks for a set amount of time.
9. Students share. If a student has taken an idea from the day's mini-lesson and elaborated further on it, I let that student share first to help emphasize the strategy.

A student sample for this lesson is provided in Figure 3.6 (page 52).

*"Push yourself to try new things—it will make you a better writer."*
*—Deborah Nourse Lattimore*

## Book: *Diary of a Worm*, by Doreen Cronin

**Day Five**

Strategy: Practicing in the notebook. Writers write diary entries.

What to do (1–7 is the mini-lesson):

1. Gather students at the meeting area with their writer's notebooks.
2. On large chart paper, create an anchor chart titled "Types of Diary Entries." The teacher explains the purpose of this strategy (to generate ideas for writing).
3. Read the book. Discuss genre, the author's purpose, time focus, connections, and information on the author's life.
4. Teacher adds his or her thoughts and ideas to the anchor chart (Think Aloud).
5. Students create a list in the **back** of their notebooks to resemble the anchor chart.
6. Students add to the list they have created. I am hoping the mentor text has helped generate some ideas for their list.
7. A couple of students share from their notebooks, and the teacher adds to the anchor chart.
8. Students write independently in the **front** of their notebooks for a set amount of time.
9. Students share  If a student has taken an idea from the day's mini-lesson and elaborated further on it, I let that student share first to help emphasize the strategy.

**Figure 3.6** Student Sample for Day Four Lesson

(Note that the student's errors have been retained for authenticity.)

Honeycup (the prences side of the story)

One upon a time a cat called cup live in the place a he loved Honey. (the food) the cats all around thought that he was not the prince and he was the boy. That was silly and now he was back at the place and the catnip ball was here and his room was ready the cats thought that they saw the prence and they were screaming "Honeycup Honeycup Honeycup." So he looked at the greatice cat ever in a dress made out of hone and he licked his paws and her name was HoneyButter when the prince walked out and greated the cat and they danced and danced and then HoneyButter ran away and and the prince ran to follow her but he cetch and went and he did and he wated for two days and went for a sherts and two girl and one in the back and the one looked the same and they lived happily ever after.

## Book: *Animals Black and White*, by Phyllis Tildes

### Day Six
Strategy: Practicing in the notebook. Writers write jokes and riddles.
What to do (1–7 is the mini-lesson):
1. Gather students at the meeting area with their writer's notebooks.
2. On large chart paper, create an anchor chart titled "How to Write a Riddle or Joke." The teacher explains the purpose of this strategy (to generate ideas for writing).
3. Read the book. Discuss genre, the author's purpose, time focus, connections, and information about the author's life.
4. Teacher adds his or her thoughts and ideas to the anchor chart (Think Aloud).
5. Students create a list in the **back** of their notebooks to resemble the anchor chart.
6. Students add to the list they have created. I am hoping the mentor text has helped generate some ideas for their list.
7. A couple of students share from their notebooks, and the teacher adds to the anchor chart.
8. Students write independently in the **front** of their notebooks for a set amount of time.
9. Students share. If a student has taken an idea from the day's mini-lesson and elaborated further on it, I let that student share first to help emphasize the strategy.

## Book: *You Have to Write*, by Janet S. Wong

### Day Seven
Strategy: Practicing in the notebook. Writers freewrite.
What to do (1–7 is the mini-lesson)
1. Gather students at the meeting area with their writer's notebooks.
2. On large chart paper, create an anchor chart titled "What Can I Write About?" The teacher explains the purpose of this strategy (to generate ideas for writing).
3. Read the book. Discuss genre, the author's purpose, time focus, connections, and information about the author's life.
4. Teacher adds his or her thoughts and ideas to anchor chart (Think Aloud).
5. Students create a list in the **back** of their notebooks to resemble the anchor chart.
6. Students add to the list they have created. I am hoping the mentor text has helped generate some ideas for their list.

7. A couple of students share from their notebooks, and the teacher adds to the anchor chart.

8. Students write independently in the **front** of their notebooks for a set amount of time.

9. Students share. If a student has taken an idea from the day's mini-lesson and elaborated further on it, I let that student share first to help emphasize the strategy.

## Book: *The Best Story*, by Eileen Spinelli

### Day Eight

Strategy: Practicing in the notebook. Writers write stories.

What to do (1–7 is the mini-lesson)

1. Gather students to meeting area with their writer's notebooks.

2. On large chart paper, create an anchor chart titled "What Makes a Good Story?" The teacher explains the purpose of this strategy (to generate ideas for writing).

3. Read the book. Discuss genre, the author's purpose, time focus, connections, and information about the author's life.

4. Teacher adds her thoughts and ideas to the anchor chart (Think Aloud).

5. Students create a list in the **back** of their notebooks to resemble the anchor chart.

6. Students add to the list they have created. I am hoping the mentor text has helped generate some ideas for their list.

7. A couple of students share from their notebooks, and the teacher adds to the anchor chart.

8. Students write independently in the **front** of their notebooks for a set amount of time.

9. Students share. If a student has taken an idea from the day's mini-lesson and elaborated further on it, I let that student share first to help emphasize the strategy.

## Book: *Everybody Needs a Rock*, by Byrd Baylor

### Day Nine

Strategy: Practicing in the notebook. Writers notice the world around them.

What to do (1–8 is the mini-lesson)

1. Gather students at the meeting area with their writer's notebooks.

2. On large chart paper, create an anchor chart titled "Noticings." The teacher explains the purpose of this strategy (to generate ideas for writing).
3. Read the book. Discuss genre, the author's purpose, time focus, connections, and information on the author's life.
4. Teacher adds his or her thoughts and ideas to the anchor chart (Think Aloud).
5. Students create a list in the **back** of their notebooks to resemble the anchor chart.
6. Teacher takes students outside to sit in a quiet place and notice their surroundings.
7. Students add to the list they have created. I am hoping the mentor text has helped generate some ideas for their list.
8. A couple of students share from their notebooks, and the teacher adds to the anchor chart.
9. Students come back inside and write independently in the **front** of their notebooks for a set amount of time.
10. Students share. If a student has taken an idea from the day's mini-lesson and elaborated further on it, I let that student share first to help emphasize the strategy.

*"Writing is like a bird-watcher watching for birds: The stories are there, you just have to train yourself to look for them."*
—*Barbara Michaels, an American author of supernatural thrillers*

## Book: *Stray*, by Cynthia Rylant

### Day Ten

Strategy: Practicing in the notebook. Writers write about animals and other topics they care about.

What to do (1–7 is the mini-lesson)

1. Gather students at the meeting area with their writer's notebooks.
2. On large chart paper, create an anchor chart titled "What I Care About." The teacher explains the purpose of this strategy (to generate ideas for writing).
3. Read the book. Discuss genre, the author's purpose, time focus, connections, and information about the author's life.
4. Teacher adds his or her thoughts and ideas to the anchor chart (Think Aloud).
5. Students create a list in the **back** of their notebooks to resemble the anchor chart.

6. Students add to the list they have created. I am hoping the mentor text has helped generate some ideas for their list.
7. A couple of students share from their notebooks, and the teacher adds to the anchor chart.
8. Students write independently in the **front** of their notebooks for a set amount of time.
9. Students share. If a student has taken an idea from the day's mini-lesson and elaborated further on it, I let that student share first to help emphasize the strategy.

*"The golden rule of writing is to write about what you care about. If you care about your topic, you'll do your best writing, and then you stand the best chance of really touching a reader in some way."*

*—Jerry Spinelli*

## Quotes for Enhancing the Practicing Lessons

- "I have had this book ever since I started to write seriously. There are 98 pages in the book. . . . And just about every one of them is filled on both sides with these so-called story ideas." —Roald Dahl

- "I save all of my idea notebooks—I have at least 50—and when I'm ready to write another book of poems I start working my way through all of the notebooks." —Jack Prelutsky

- "Writing is 90 percent listening. The deeper you listen, the better you write." —Natalie Goldberg

- "Writers live twice. In a rainstorm everyone quickly runs down the street with umbrellas, raincoats, and newspapers over their heads. Writers go back outside in the rain with a notebook in front of them in hand. They look at the puddles; watch them fill; watch the rain splash in them." —Natalie Goldberg

- "The golden rule of writing is to write about what you care about. If you care about your topic, you'll do your best writing, and then you stand the best chance of really touching a reader in some way." —Jerry Spinelli

- "Push yourself to try new things; it will make you a better writer."                    —Deborah Nourse Lattimore

- "You're never going to be a writer unless you write. You have to sit down and write."                    —Jane Yolen

- "Write, write, and write some more. Think of writing as a muscle that needs lots of exercise."                    —Jane Yolen

## Chapter Four

# Collecting and Selecting Ideas in the Writer's Notebook

"If you breathe, if you live, you have something to write about."
—Donald Graves

Writers are collectors. We never use all of the information we have, but we have it just in case. Some of the information that has been collected becomes ideas for a story, a poem, or just about any other type of writing. All of this information is salvaged in the writer's notebook. In this chapter, I want to show you how to open up the world of collecting and selecting to your students.

## Step One: Collecting

It is a good idea to brainstorm with your students the types of information they can collect in their notebooks. (See Figure 4.1 on page 59 for a sample.) I like to make an anchor chart and display it in an area of the room where it can be easily read and added to, much like the writing smorgasbord chart discussed in Chapter Three.

### *Collecting with Artifacts*

At the beginning of the year, I bring out an old battered shoebox filled with bits and pieces of my life. I enjoy showing my students the postcard from France that my granny sent me roughly 25 years

**Figure 4.1**  Collecting in the Notebook

- Memorable lines or quotes from books
- Pictures from magazines or from home
- Interesting words
- Newspaper clippings
- Snatches of conversations
- Web sites
- Questions about topics of interest
- Setting ideas
- Notes about close observations
- Great first lines for things you'd like to write, for chapters, short stories, poems, etc.
- Lists of possible character names
- Magazine articles on subjects that interest you
- Editorials
- Birthday or inspirational greeting cards

ago. I have a sample of both my daughters' baby blankets and a hair bow I made for my youngest daughter at Halloween. One of my absolute treasures is a small blue paper leaf with the word *mom* written on it. When my oldest daughter was four, she went to a teacher's afterschool meeting with me. As we were filling out our name tags, she looked to me and said, "Mom, I already have yours done for you." And so she did. I wore that little blue leaf with pride, and when it was time for me to stand up and introduce myself, I enjoyed the opportunity to share my "mom moment" with the other teachers. I want my students to see the value in the simple things in life and how those moments can make the best writing ideas. I ask each of my students bring in a shoebox, and as the year progresses, they bring in and collect artifacts that will inspire them to write and think of ideas to write about.

## *Collecting through Mentor Texts*

The other way we collect is through mentor texts. I believe that classroom bookshelves should be filled with books that children love, and teachers can't wait to read. During the collecting step of the process, our writer's workshop has a different feel to it. It is one of discovery, the discovery of an idea or topic that may make the journey to publication. Now that my students (with me right beside them) have practiced and played around with the entries in our notebooks, we are ready to get a little more serious about the possibilities and purpose of the notebooks with regards to publication. Publication is not the key here—the writing process is. Our mantra is, "Value the process; process over product." When we collect with mentor texts we use the **back** of the notebook. The front is still reserved for freewriting and exploring and playing with words: practice before the big game . . . publication. The following two lessons are examples of our step-by-step procedures in the writing workshop. One lesson sample is for narrative writing and the other is for an expository essay. I have included additional lessons and student samples at the end of this chapter.

I use several strategies when teaching my students how to collect from mentor texts:

- Webbing
- Listing
- Writing back
- T-charts
- Timelines
- ABC charts
- Column charts
- Quick sketches

Many of these strategies will be used again when students begin to marinate on an idea or topic they have chosen to write about. (Marinating is covered in Chapter Five.)

## Lesson Sample: Collecting for Narrative Writing

### Book: *The Relatives Came*, by Cynthia Rylant

**Day One**

Strategy: Listing

What to do (1–8 is the mini-lesson):

1. Gather students at the meeting area with their writer's notebooks.
2. On large chart paper, create an anchor chart titled "A Time You Had Visitors." The teacher explains the purpose of this strategy (to generate ideas for writing) and names it (a list).
3. Read the book. Discuss genre, the author's purpose, time focus, connections, and information about the author's life.

4. Teacher adds his or her thoughts and ideas to anchor chart (Think Aloud).
5. Students create a list in the **back** of their notebooks to resemble the anchor chart.
6. Students add to the list they have created. I am hoping the mentor text has helped generate some ideas for their list (Try-it).
7. Students are then asked to turn to an elbow partner and share what they just wrote in their notebooks.
8. A couple of students share from their notebooks, and the teacher adds responses to the anchor chart.
9. Students go to their special spots and continue to add to the list. When students feel they have a good grasp of creating visitor topics, they may continue writing in the **front** of the notebooks for the remainder of independent writing time.
10. Students share. If a student has taken an idea from the day's mini-lesson and elaborated further on it, I let that student share first to help emphasize the strategy.

A student sample for this lesson is shown in Figure 4.2 (page 62).

## Lesson Sample: Collecting for Expository Writing

### Book: *Girls*, by Maya Ajmera

**Day One**

Strategy: Column chart (adjective/who/why)

What to do (1–8 is the mini-lesson)

1. Gather students at the meeting area with their writer's notebooks.
2. On chart paper, create an anchor chart titled "Adjective/Who/Why." The teacher explains the purpose of the strategy (to generate topics and details for an expository topic) and names the strategy (column chart).
3. Read excerpts from the book. Discuss genre, the author's purpose, time focus, connections, and information on the author's life.
4. Teacher adds his or her thoughts and ideas to the anchor chart (Think Aloud).
5. Students create a chart in the **back** of their notebooks to resemble the anchor chart.

**Figure 4.2** Collecting Sample for Day One

(Note that the student's errors have been retained for authenticity.)

| | |
|---|---|
| | (Listing) A Time you had visitors |
| • | I went to my best friend s house for the night. |
| • | Our grandparents came over for our birthday. |
| • | We went to our grandparents for Thanksgiving. and Chrismas. |
| • | I go to my friends house a lot. |
| • | Our grandma came to spend the night. |
| • | My best friend came to our house to spend the night. |
| • | I went to my friend. koreys house. and he came to mine. |
| • | My grandparents came over for Mamoreial day and brought KFC. |
| | |
| | |
| | |
| | |
| | |
| | |
| | |
| | |
| | |
| | |
| | |
| | |
| | |
| | |
| | |
| | |
| | |

6. Students add to the chart they have created. I am hoping my examples and the mentor text has helped generate some ideas and details for their own chart (Try-it).
7. Students are then asked to turn to an elbow partner and share what they just wrote in their notebooks.
8. A couple of students share from their notebooks, and the teacher adds responses to the anchor chart.
9. Students go to their special spots and continue to add to the column chart. When students feel they have a good grasp of creating topics about people they know or want to know more about, they may continue writing in the **front** of the notebook for the remainder of independent writing time.
10. Students share. If a student has taken an idea from the day's mini-lesson and elaborated further on it, I let that student share first to help emphasize the strategy.

## Why Collect? Choice Equals Voice

I am often asked, "What is the real purpose for collecting?" In my classroom, we rarely use prompts to decide what it is we are going to write about. Because of this, I need to show my students how to find their own ideas and topics. This is where collecting comes in. A few years ago, I came across two quotes that had great influence over the way I taught writing. The first is from Vicki Spandel, developer of the 6 Trait model for writing:

> *"Teachers often ask, 'Why don't students put more **voice** in their writing?' The same reason caged animals don't run more!"*

I wondered, after reading this quote, how many students I had "caged" with prompt writing? I understand the importance of writing on demand, but this cannot be the only exposure a student has. My rule of thumb is this: after completing a unit of study I assign my students a timed prompt, much like they will see on the state writing test. By going through the process first, with me guiding them and laying a foundation, they will have had the opportunity to select their own idea, marinate on it, draft it, and then see the process through to publication.

There is a comfort in immersing oneself into a mode of writing and having the opportunity to read and hear literature examples, conference with the teacher throughout the process, receive feedback from peers, and finalize the study through sharing. At that point, the thought of an assigned prompt is not such a dread. When teachers continuously assign prompt writing it is, as Donald Murray says, like "writing welfare." We have given everything to the students. The challenge to think and dig deep into their lives is no longer needed. In return we have also taken away the freedom to explore one's life, both the good and the bad. I have had many experiences that validate the importance of choice, and I would like to share two.

A couple of years ago, there was a boy in my class who came to me with very little desire to write. Many days he simply refused. I didn't give up. We were working on a personal narrative unit and were collecting moments from our lives we could write about. During our conferencing one day, he looked at me and began to cry . . . sob. I sat down and simply asked him to tell me what he was feeling. He explained that his father had died four years earlier, and he wanted to write about it. This sadness had been stored in him for a long time. I realized that I had awakened the freedom for him to dig deep and search out those moments in his life that he needed to revisit. Through our conversation, he began to talk about the last time his father had helped him ride his new bike. He was heading straight for a brick wall when his father came to his rescue and stopped him from crashing. His father died several days later. This precious child had bottled that up, and now he popped the cork and let the memories flow. His personal narrative was filled with emotion and memories. I was forever touched, as was everyone in the classroom. From that point on, we knew to keep tissues handy at all times. We were a community of writers learning to trust each other. I have never seen a prompt that would allow that type of personal release, and I doubt it exists.

The following quote from Irish-American teacher and Pulitzer Prize-winning writer Frank McCourt also gave me validation on my decision to step away from prompts. It was risky, and I felt a little uncomfortable at first, but now I will never go back to teaching the old way again.

> *"I can't think of anything like the other students talk about, the family car, Dad's old baseball mitt, the sled they had so much fun on, and the kitchen table they did their homework on. All I can think of is the bed I share with three brothers and even though I am ashamed of it, I have to write about it."*
> *—Frank McCourt*

When teachers ask students to write about summer vacations many may have very little to say. The school in which I teach has a high free-and-reduced lunch population, and many of these students come from single-parent homes. If prompts are focused around a favorite gift or a trip with the family (or a summer vacation), many of our students are left without the experiential background needed to feel successful with these types of prompts. However, when the focus of the writer's workshop is choice of ideas and topics, and any idea can be written in the notebook, students begin to feel ownership of their writing. In a nutshell, choice equals voice, and when students are given this opportunity they flourish as writers.

It is here I would like to share my next story with you: My class and I were revisiting the personal narrative. This time we were focusing on action, danger, and mistakes that caused harm to us or someone we loved. I read the mentor text *Short Cut*, by Donald Crews, to elaborate on this idea. Now, you know, the boys loved this particular collecting lesson. Anyway, as we moved to our special writing spots, one of my students, a very shy child with many family issues, just sat at the meeting area. I sat there with him for a minute to see what he would do next. He turned to a page in the front of his notebook, his freewriting, and simply pointed to an entry. I sat next to him and read a touching short story about the death of his beloved bird. As tears welled up in his eyes, he asked me if I would please read this to the class. I said I would and called for everyone's attention and read his entry. As I read, my other students began to come forward and join us at the carpet. When I finished reading, he looked around at all of us and said, "I have never told anyone this, but it is my fault my bird is dead. As we were leaving to go to school I put him back in his cage and forgot to lock it. While we were gone, he flew out and hit our wall and I found him dead that afternoon. I never told my mom it was me who didn't lock the cage." It was his desire to choose that moment in his life as the basis for his personal narrative. Our collecting that day (on danger and harm to others or ourselves) had resurfaced this moment in his life. He had captured it briefly in his notebook, and then revisited the moment and wrote an incredibly touching piece. Just like Frank McCourt, this child felt shame but had to write about it. This is what a writing workshop offers, and this is what choice creates.

## Beginning the Process in Your Own Classroom

At this point, I would like you give you a timeline of how long we practice, collect, and so forth. See Figure 4.3 on page 66. I hope this will give you a framework for how to begin planning your units of study. I will take you from the beginning of the year all the way through a personal narrative unit of study and then through an expository one.

**Figure 4.3** The First 80 Days (or so...)

Establishing procedure and routines: 5–7 days
Introducing the notebook lessons: 10 days
Collecting personal narrative ideas: 10–12 days
Rereading our notebooks /notebook dig: 1–2 days
Selecting an idea: 1–2 days
Marinating on the idea: 3–4 days
Drafting: 2–3 days
Revising: 2–3 days
Editing: 1–2 days
Publishing: 1–2 days
Whole class celebration (sharing): 1–2 days
Timed personal narrative (with a prompt): 1 day
Collecting expository topics: 10–12 days
Rereading our notebooks/notebook dig: 1–2 days
Selecting a topic: 1–2 days
Marinating on the topic: 3–4 days
Drafting: 2–3 days
Revising: 2–3 days
Editing: 1–2 days
Publishing: 1–2 days
Whole class celebration (sharing): 1–2 days
Timed expository essay (with a prompt): 1 day

This timeline is not set in stone, thus the ranges in days for each step. But it does give a clear pattern for routines, and that is important because students do well with predictability.

## Selecting: Narrowing Down the Options

Selecting an idea sounds so simple, yet when my students (or I) try to narrow down the options, it can be difficult. For many students, the only real control they have had over their writing has been how they planned to respond to a prompt. In my classroom, I am giving them freedom, and this can actually be more difficult than merely assigning.

Through trial and error, I have found a method that makes "selecting" understandable, manageable, and exciting for my students. This is where all of our hard work collecting comes to fruition; we now get to choose.

### Begin with a Notebook Dig

To begin with, we take two days to reread our individual writer's notebooks. I like to refer to this as a "notebook dig." I tell my students that, just as archaeologists dig for buried treasures, for these next two days, we are going to dig for treasures of a different kind: ideas. During this time, my students use a highlighter to mark potential entries from their personal collecting charts found in the back of their notebooks that may have potential (a seed idea) for a future piece of writing.

I always enjoy starting the year with personal narratives, so most of the collecting charts that my students have at this point are geared towards that particular unit of study. Another way to spark interest in selecting an idea is to allow students to swap notebooks and enjoy each other's entries. My students love reading each others' notebooks. It is rewarding seeing how proud everyone is. The energy in the room is addictive. During this time, I conference and listen in on my students talking like writers. When Susan tells Jill, "I love how descriptive your memory web is. It made me think of more ideas to add to mine," I can't help but smile and know that the process is working.

After a day or so of sharing, my students are ready for the exciting moment of selecting a seed idea, one that will grow through the journey of publication. The steps we use to select are the same with any unit of study we may be working on. Since this book is based on personal narrative and expository writing, I will continue to focus on these two areas.

### Ideas or Topics: What's the Difference?

I would like to point out that when we are working on narrative writing, I use the word *idea* throughout my lessons and information. When I am referring to expository writing, the word *topic* is used. Why do I do this? It makes clear to my students that these types of writing are very different. The process is the same and our procedure for selecting an idea or topic is very similar, but the end result of the writing is different. The voice is different, and the collecting strategies look a little different.

### Selecting for Narrative Writing

It would be an ideal world if we could look at our students and say to them, "OK, pick an idea to write on" and they would do it. I have tried that, and it didn't exactly work for me. So I came up with a list of questions that, as writers, we could ask ourselves, to help us through the process. I am going to take you into my classroom for just a moment and let you listen in on this lesson:

**Me:** Good morning students!! I am so excited because today we get to select a personal narrative idea from our notebooks. I know that we have all worked so hard with collecting, and so the real challenge will be to narrow down all of our wonderful choices. The first thing I would like you to do is look back through your notebook for a minute. Look at the highlighted areas you focused on the last couple of days.

It is important that I give my students a few minutes to flip through their notebooks. I then pick up my notebook and say the following:

**Me:** I would like everyone to look at me for just a minute. I want to show you my notebook and the highlighted entries in it. You will notice that I found a lot of ideas from the heart-map lesson. I also found some potential narrative ideas in my memory web. I want you to watch what I do next; I am going to 'think aloud' this process, so listen carefully.

**Me (Thinking Aloud):** Hmmm . . . when I look at my heart map I see that I have highlighted the following: Labrador retrievers, scuba diving, Mexican food, and my daughters. From the memory web I highlighted Walter's death and graduating from college. I am going to select three of these ideas and write them down on this sticky note. I want to make sure I leave myself space for my checking system.

At this point, I create a larger model of my sticky note on the whiteboard. It can be seen in Figure 4.4 (below).

**Me (Thinking Aloud):** Now, before I ask myself these questions, I'd better make sure I have personal narrative ideas on my sticky note. OK, I really love Mexican food, but I can't say I have ever had an experience that evokes lots of feelings and emotions. I can't think of a potential story about this idea. I actually think that this would be

**Figure 4.4**  My Selecting Example

```
_____  Mexican food
_____  Scuba diving
_____  Labrador retrievers
```

better suited for an expository essay. I could explain how Mexican food is made, the history behind some favorite dishes, etc. So I think I may have to select another option from my collecting.

I am now role playing and looking through my notebook again with the highlighter in my hand.

> **Me (Thinking Aloud):** Aha, I think I found something. I put buttermilk biscuits in my heart map, and I have a really good story about that. Let me erase Mexican food and put buttermilk biscuits in its place. I sure am glad I am testing out these ideas.

Figure 4.5 (below) shows my re-created visual.

> **Me (Thinking Aloud):** I'd better test the other two before I start narrowing down. Let's see . . . scuba diving . . . oh, yes. I have lots of stories about that. I really think everyone will enjoy the one about the shark. I will keep this one on my list. Let me rethink Labrador retrievers. Oh, my, I have so many stories from my rescue days . . . yep, this one will do nicely, too. This might be a good time to write about Walter, the senior Lab who lost his fight with heart worms. You know, now that I look at it, these ideas could really form into any mode of writing, that's nice to remember for later. I can recycle and use them for poetry or expository, or even a memoir. It's sure nice to know that this collecting is really going to help me anytime I write.

It is critical that students see teachers walking the same path that they are about to be asked to walk. My mini-lesson this day is simply centered on me role playing and thinking out loud. Let's keep going because I have more to show you.

> **Me:** Is everyone following my process right now? Can you "see" me thinking? I want you to write three potential ideas on your sticky note and be sure to add the line for our checking system.

This takes a few moments. During this time I am walking around monitoring and showing support.

> **Me:** I would like for everyone to test out their ideas just like I did with the Mexican food. I will give you a couple of minutes to do this.
> [A few minutes pass.]
> What a great job you are doing, why don't you turn to an elbow partner and tell them a little about your three selections.

**Figure 4.5** My Collecting Sample

| | |
|---|---|
| _____ | Buttermilk biscuits |
| _____ | Scuba diving |
| _____ | Labrador retrievers |

It is vital for students to get the chance to talk during this process. Talking is thinking, and I want them to do lots of thinking. This is one of my favorite times to eavesdrop because the excitement is beginning to build and it is apparent in their conversations.

**Me:** Excellent, excellent. We are almost ready to select. Let me take you back to my example on the board and, once again, let you see me think this through. I want you to listen as I ask myself these five questions. My hope is that this process of questioning myself will help me narrow down which idea to write my personal narrative on.

Then I display a larger version of the question chart that will be glued in the back of their notebooks. (See Figure 4.6, below, for an example.) I like for my students to glue in vital learning tools so that later in the year, they become independent in this process.

I want to show you, step by step, how I figured out which idea to write my personal narrative on. I looked at my three choices on the sticky note, and for every time I could honestly answer "yes," I gave that idea an X. The idea with the most Xs is the one I am going to write about this time. It doesn't mean that I will never have the opportunity to write about the other ideas, but those stories may come at another time. So here I go . . .

**1. Are there strong feelings and emotions surrounding this idea?**

**Me (Thinking Aloud):** I would have to say no to the buttermilk biscuits. I certainly enjoyed eating them, but no real emotions or feelings were taking place that I remember. But you bet I had feelings of fright and excitement during my scuba diving adventure and happiness and sadness with regards to my Lab rescue and Labrador retrievers. I'd better mark those two.

**Figure 4.6** Questioning Chart

---

**Do I Have a Good Idea?**

1. Are there strong feelings and emotions surrounding this idea?
2. Do I remember many details, and will I be able to describe them?
3. Do I feel my audience will be interested in my idea?
4. Is this idea important to me? Is it important enough that I will work hard each day to elaborate on it?
5. Am I excited to write about this idea?

---

Figure 4.7 (below) shows my updated visual.

## 2. Do I remember many details, and will I be able to describe them?

> **Me (Thinking Aloud):** I was pretty young when my babysitter made those homemade biscuits, but I can remember lots of details like how the Crisco can shone in the sun and how the butter formed a perfect circle on my napkin . . . I feel good about marking this one.
> My scuba adventure with the shark is filled with vivid details so this one gets an X too. As far as the Labrador retriever choice, you bet I can describe those details with great clarity. I will mark each of these ideas.

Now my sticky note looks like Figure 4.8 (below).

As I continue to ask myself questions, I begin to narrow down which choice I will write my personal narrative on. I know this seems like an exhausting process, but the students love it and appreciate the end result. I typically have to hold their hands through this selecting step one time, and then they have it. (See Figure 4.9, page 72, for a final student sample.) Ultimately the process led me to select and write about my scuba diving experience with a shark. Question number three, audience interest, sealed the deal with that one.

**Figure 4.7**   My Selecting Sample

| | |
|---|---|
| _____ | Buttermilk biscuits |
| __X__ | Scuba diving |
| __X__ | Labrador retrievers |

**Figure 4.8**   My Updated Selecting Sample

| | |
|---|---|
| __XX__ | Buttermilk biscuits |
| __XX__ | Scuba diving |
| __XX__ | Labrador retrievers |

**Figure 4.9**    A Final Selecting Sample

Do I Have a Good Idea?
1. Are there strong feelings and emotions surrounding this idea?
2. Do I remember many details and will I be able to describe them?
3. Do I feel my audience will be interested in my idea?
4. Is this idea important to me? Important enough to work hard each day to elaborate?
5. Am I excited about writing to this idea?

| ✔✔ | Trees |
| ✔✔✔✔ | Science |
| ✔✔ | Steak |

| ✔✔ | I got my tonsils out |
| ✔✔ | The pool party |
| ✔✔✔✔✔ | Scariest moment |

| ✔✔ | went to the movies |
| ✔✔✔✔✔ | shot my first hunting gun |
| ✔✔✔✔✔ | found a 100 dollar bill on the ground |

**Figure 4.10**   Do I Have a Good Topic?

Ask yourself these questions:

1. Am I passionate or opinionated about this topic?
2. Do I already know many facts about this particular topic?
3. Could I teach someone about this topic?
4. Am I prepared to do research if necessary?
5. Do I feel my audience will be interested in this topic?

## Selecting for Expository Writing

When we are selecting a topic for an expository piece, the same step-by-step process is modeled, yet a different series of questions is asked. Figure 4.10 (above) shows the question chart we use to help select an expository topic. Remember, an expository piece of writing is more about explaining to the reader, where a narrative piece is about entertaining the reader.

At this point my students and I have selected our idea for a personal narrative (and if you are following my first 80-day framework, an expository topic will follow soon). It is time to start marinating. This is what Chapter Five is all about.

## What if There Is a Tie?

Let's talk about ties before I end this chapter. First, yes, sometimes there will be a tie in the selection process. That is fine. Just have the student think a little deeper about the questions, and this should help narrow it down further. Sometimes taking a moment with the student while the others are working, and allowing the student to talk out the choices, will help that student make a decision.

Once we have selected our ideas, I create a large anchor chart with everyone's name and idea out beside it, and you can bet I add mine right up there with theirs. You see, I am doing exactly what it is I am asking my students to do, all the way to the finish line (publication). I am not going to ask them to do anything I don't do.

## Making It Real: Real Authors Collect and Select

I would like to share some thought-provoking quotes about collecting and selecting. As stated earlier, I use quotes alongside my lessons in every step of the writing process to enhance the mini-lesson for the day. I feel that the more students can hear the voices of other writers, the more embedded the curriculum will become to them.

- "Writing, I think is not apart from living. Writing is a kind of double living. The writer experiences everything twice."
  —Catherine Drinker Bowen

- "Begin with 'I remember.' Write lots of small memories. If you fall into one large memory, write that. Don't be concerned if the memory happened five seconds or five years ago."
  —Natalie Goldberg

- "How to generate writing ideas, things to write about? Whatever's in front of you is a good beginning. Then move out into the streets. You can go anyplace. Tell me everything you know. Own anything you want in your writing and then let it go."
  —Natalie Goldberg

## Additional Narrative Collecting Lessons

### Book: *Fly Away Home*, by Eve Bunting

**Day Two**
Strategy: T-chart
What to do (1–7 is the mini-lesson):

1. Gather students at the meeting area with their writer's notebooks.
2. On large chart paper, create an anchor chart titled "I Wonder/I Wish." The teacher explains the purpose of this strategy (to generate ideas for writing) and names it (a T- chart).
3. Read the book. Discuss genre, the author's purpose, time focus, connections, and information about the author's life.
4. Teacher adds his or her thoughts and ideas to the anchor chart (Think Aloud).

5. Students create a T-chart in the **back** of their notebooks to resemble the anchor chart.
6. Students add to the T-chart they have created. I am hoping the mentor text has helped generate some ideas for their T-chart.
7. A couple of students share from their notebooks, and the teacher adds to the anchor chart.
8. Students write independently in the **front** of their notebooks for a set amount of time.
9. Students share. If a student has taken an idea from the day's mini-lesson and elaborated further on it, I let that student share first to help emphasize the strategy.

A student sample for this lesson is shown in Figure 4.11 (page 76).

## Book: *An Angel for Solomon Singer,* by Cynthia Rylant

### Day Three

Strategy: T-chart (added to the one from the day-two lesson)

What to do (1–6 is the mini-lesson):

1. Gather students at the meeting area with their writer's notebooks.
2. The teacher refers back to the "I Wonder/I Wish" chart from day two. The teacher explains the purpose of this strategy (to generate ideas for writing) and names it (a T-chart).
3. Read the book. Discuss genre, the author's purpose, time focus, connections, and information about the author's life.
4. Teacher adds his or her thoughts and ideas to the anchor chart (Think Aloud).
5. Students review the T-chart in the **back** of their notebooks that they worked on the day before. Students add to the T-chart they previously created. I am hoping the mentor text has helped generate some more ideas for their T-chart.
6. A couple of students share from their notebooks, and the teacher adds to the anchor chart.
7. Students write independently in the **front** of their notebooks for a set amount of time.
8. Students share. If a student has taken an idea from the days mini-lesson and elaborated further on it, I let that student share first to help emphasize the strategy.

**Figure 4.11** Student Sample for Day Two of Collecting

(Note that the student's errors have been retained for authenticity.)

| | I wonder | I wish |
|---|---|---|
| | • Why leaves turn orange in the fall? | • Maddie Mills would move back. |
| | • If spring feels like fall? | • Summer wasn't as hot as it always is. |
| | • If lights can spark a toaster? | • The YMCA wasn't so pricey. |
| | • Why the Sydney funnel Spyder is so poisinious? | • I could get peace and quiet in math. |
| | • Why lonely people can't seem to find friends? Or have them but are still upset? | • I could go owling. |
| | • Why some people are so talkative? | • I could go to my cousin's house more. |
| | • Why can't I be quiet at home? | |

## Book: *My Rotten Redheaded Older Brother,* by Patricia Polacco

Day Four

Strategy: Writing Back

**Reminder: excerpt from p. 25 of Stephen King's book *On Writing* is copied on chart paper**

What to do (1–7 is the mini-lesson):

1. Gather students at the meeting area with their writer's notebooks.
2. On chart paper, create and anchor chart titled "Writing Back." Read the excerpt from King's book. The teacher explains the process of Writing Back (thinking back as far as you can) as well as its purpose (to generate ideas), and names the strategy (Writing Back).
3. Read the book. Discuss genre, the author's purpose, time focus, connections, and information about the author's life.
4. Teacher adds his or her thoughts and ideas to the anchor chart (Think Aloud).
5. Students create a page in the **back** of their notebooks to resemble the anchor chart.
6. Students add to the page they have created. I am hoping the mentor text has helped generate some ideas for their notebook page.
7. A couple of students share from their notebooks, and the teacher adds to the anchor chart.
8. Students write independently in the **front** of their notebooks for a set amount of time.
9. Students share. If a student has taken an idea from the day's mini-lesson and elaborated further on it, I let that student share first to help emphasize the strategy.

Stephen King Excerpt:

> Let's get one thing straight right now, shall we? There is no Idea Dump, no Story Central, no Island of the Buried Bestsellers; good story ideas seem to come quite literally from nowhere, sailing at you right out of the empty sky: two previously unrelated ideas come together and make something new under the sun. Your job isn't to find these ideas but to recognize them when they show up.

A student sample from this lesson is shown in Figure 4.12 (page 78).

**Figure 4.12** Student Sample for Day Four of Collecting

(Note that the student's errors have been retained for authenticity.)

| Age | Writing Back |
|---|---|
| 7 | I used to follow kevin and Brandon everywhere to play. |
| 9 | A spyder got super close to my face. |
| 8 | The day I adopted Hunter. |
| 7-8 | The day I went to my cousins. |
| 6-7 | The day Mesha died. |
| 7 | When Pasha got put to sleep. |
| 8 | The day Ana died. |
| ??? | Christmas morning when I got my hamster. |
| 6-7 | When I was introduced to Pokemon. |
| 8-9 | When I first met Ella. |
| 9 | When Mom told me I might have to get ride of Hunter. Not likely though. |
| 8-9 | Mom gave Hunter the nickname 'Boo boo kitty' |
| 9 | When Ella introduced me to Warriors. |
| 9 | When Ella, Meg, and I started a clan together. |
| 9 | When Ella and Taylor spent the night. |

## Book: *Owl Moon*, by Jane Yolen

### Day Five

Strategy: Writing Back (added to the one from the day-four lesson)

What to do (1–6 is the mini-lesson):

1. Gather students at the meeting area with their writer's notebooks.
2. The teacher refers back to "Writing Back," the chart from day four. The teacher explains the purpose of this strategy (to generate ideas for writing) and names it (Writing Back).
3. Read the book. Discuss genre, the author's purpose, time focus, connections, and information about the author's life.
4. Teacher adds his or her thoughts and ideas to the anchor chart (Think Aloud).
5. Students review the page in the **back** of their notebooks that they worked on the day before. Students add to the page they previously created. I am hoping the mentor text has helped generate some ideas for their notebook page.
6. A couple of students share from their notebooks, and the teacher adds to the anchor chart.
7. Students write independently in the **front** of their notebooks for a set amount of time.
8. Students share. If a student has taken an idea from the day's mini-lesson and elaborated further on it, I let that student share first to help emphasize the strategy.

## Book: *The Wall*, by Eve Bunting

### Day Six

Strategy: Webbing

What to do (1–7 is the mini-lesson):

1. Gather students at the meeting area with their writer's notebooks.
2. On large chart paper, create an anchor chart titled "Memories." The teacher explains the purpose of this strategy (to generate ideas for writing) and names it (Webbing).
3. Read the book. Discuss genre, the author's purpose, time focus, connections, and information about the author's life.
4. Teacher adds his or her thoughts and ideas to the anchor chart (Think Aloud).

5. Students create a web in the **back** of their notebooks to resemble the anchor chart.
6. Students add to the web they have created. I am hoping the mentor text has helped generate some ideas for their web.
7. A couple of students share from their notebooks, and the teacher adds to the anchor chart.
8. Students write independently in the **front** of their notebooks for a set amount of time.
9. Students share. If a student has taken an idea from the day's mini-lesson and elaborated further on it, I let that student share first to help emphasize the strategy.

## Book: *The Secret Knowledge of Grown-Ups,* by David Wisniewski

**Day Seven**

Strategy: Webbing

What to do (1–7 is the mini-lesson):

1. Gather students at the meeting area with their writer's notebooks.
2. On large chart paper, create an anchor chart titled "Rules." The teacher explains the purpose of this strategy (to generate ideas for writing) and names it (Webbing). The focus will be on a time students either broke or followed a rule.
3. Read the book. Discuss genre, the author's purpose, time focus, connections, and information about the author's life.
4. Teacher adds his or her thoughts and ideas to the anchor chart (Think Aloud).
5. Students create a web in the **back** of their notebooks to resemble the anchor chart.
6. Students add to the web they have created. I am hoping the mentor text has helped generate some ideas for their web.
7. A couple of students share from their notebooks, and the teacher adds to the anchor chart.
8. Students write independently in the **front** of their notebooks for a set amount of time.
9. Students share. If a student has taken an idea from the day's mini-lesson and elaborated further on it, I let that student share first to help emphasize the strategy.

A student sample for this lesson is shown in Figure 4.13 (page 81).

**Figure 4.13**    Student Sample for Day Seven of Collecting

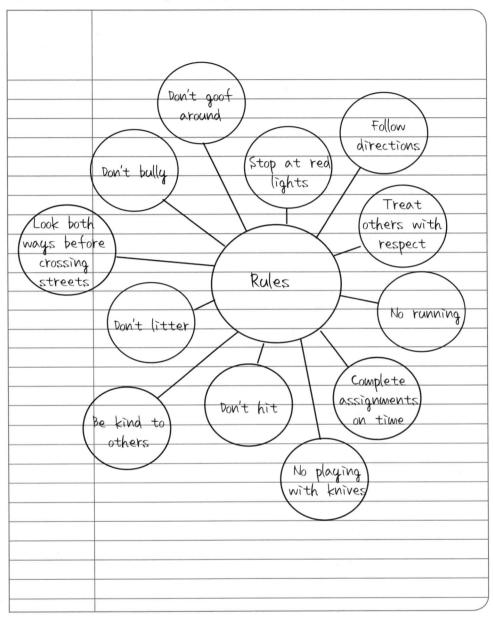

## Book: *Hello Ocean*, by Pam Muñoz Ryan

### Day Eight

Strategy: Sensory Detail Columns

What to do (1–7 is the mini-lesson):

1. Gather students at the meeting area with their writer's notebooks.
2. On large chart paper, create an anchor chart titled "Sensory Details." The teacher explains the purpose of this strategy (to identify and use our five senses for detailed writing) and names it (Sensory Detail Columns).
3. Read the book. Discuss genre, the author's purpose, time focus, connections, and information about the author's life.
4. Teacher adds his or her thoughts and ideas to the anchor chart (Think Aloud).
5. Students create columns (five of them) in the **back** of their notebooks to resemble the anchor chart.
6. Students add to the columns they have created. I am hoping the mentor text has helped generate the use of senses in their writing.
7. A couple of students share from their notebooks, and the teacher adds to the anchor chart.
8. Students write independently in the **front** of their notebooks for a set amount of time.
9. Students share. If a student has taken an idea from the day's mini-lesson and elaborated further on it, I let that student share first to help emphasize the strategy.

A sample of a five-column anchor chart for this lesson is shown in Figure 4.14 (page 83).

## Book: *Night in the Country*, Cynthia Rylant

### Day Nine

Strategy: Sensory Detail Columns (added to the one from the day-eight lesson)

What to do (1–6 is the mini-lesson):

1. Gather students at the meeting area with their writer's notebooks.
2. The teacher refers back to "Sensory Details," the chart from day eight. The teacher explains the purpose of this strategy (to identify and use our five senses for detailed writing) and names it (Sensory Detail Columns).
3. Read the book. Discuss genre, the author's purpose, time focus, connections, and information about the author's life

**Figure 4.14** Sensory Details Chart

| | | | | |
|---|---|---|---|---|
| | | | | |

4. Teacher adds his or her thoughts and ideas to the anchor chart (Think Aloud).
5. Students review the columns in the **back** of their notebooks they worked on the day before. Students add to the columns they previously created. I am hoping the mentor text has helped generate some more use of the senses in their writing.
6. A couple of students share from their notebooks, and the teacher adds to the anchor chart.
7. Students write independently in the **front** of their notebooks for a set amount of time.
8. Students share. If a student has taken an idea from the day's mini-lesson and elaborated further on it, I let that student share first to help emphasize the strategy.

A student sample for this lesson is shown in Figure 4.15 (page 85).

## Book: *My Mama Had a Dancing Heart*, by Libba Moore Gray

### Day Ten
Strategy: Heart Map
What to do (1–7 is the mini-lesson):
1. Gather students at the meeting area with their writer's notebooks.
2. On large chart paper, create an anchor chart in the shape of a large heart titled "What I Love." The teacher explains the purpose of this strategy (to generate ideas for writing) and names it (a Heart Map).
3. Read the book. Discuss genre, the author's purpose, time focus, connections, and information about the author's life.
4. Teacher adds his or her thoughts and ideas to the anchor chart (Think Aloud).
5. Students create a Heart Map in the **back** of their notebooks to resemble the anchor chart.
6. Students add to the Heart Map they have created. I am hoping the mentor text has helped generate some ideas for their Heart Map.
7. A couple of students share from their notebooks, and the teacher adds to the anchor chart.
8. Students write independently in the **front** of their notebooks for a set amount of time.
9. Students share. If a student has taken an idea from the day's mini-lesson and elaborated further on it, I let that student share first to help emphasize the strategy.

**Figure 4.15**  Student Sample for Day Nine of Collecting

(Note that the student's errors have been retained for authenticity.)

| Object | Touch Word |
|---|---|
| Cat tongue | Verry rough |
| Silly Putty | Slimy |
| Eye buger | Gooshy and crusty |
| Smoothie | Lumpy |
| Earaser | Smooth and soft |
| Feather | Fluffy |
| Sand | Soft and scratchy |
| Wolf | Soft |
| Skunk | Soft |
| Old Paint | Glumpy |
| Sand Dollar | Smooth |
| Dog Slobber | Wet and slimy |
| Puzzle | Bumpy |
| Bone | Hard |
| Water Melon | Smuchy |
| Snow | CCOOLLDD |
| Fire | Smushy |
| Puding | Scratchy |
| Sweater | Soft |
| Carpet | |

## Book: *All the Place to Love*, by Patricia MacLachlan

### Day Eleven

Strategy: Heart Map (added to the one from the day-ten lesson)

What to do (1–6 is the mini-lesson)

1. Gather students at the meeting area with their writer's notebooks.
2. The teacher refers back to "What I Love," the heart-shaped chart from day ten. The teacher reviews the purpose of this strategy (to generate ideas for writing) and names it (a Heart Map).
3. Read the book. Discuss genre, the author's purpose, time focus, connections, and information about the author's life.
4. Teacher adds his or her thoughts and ideas to the anchor chart (Think Aloud).
5. Students review the Heart Map in the **back** of their notebooks that they worked on the day before. Students add to the Heart Map they previously created. I am hoping the mentor text has helped generate some more ideas for their Heart Map.
6. A couple of students share from their notebooks, and the teacher adds to the anchor chart.
7. Students write independently in the **front** of their notebooks for a set amount of time.
8. Students share. If a student has taken an idea from the day's mini-lesson and elaborated further on it, I let the student share first to help emphasize the strategy.

## Book: *Nothing Ever Happens on 90th Street*, by Roni Schotter

### Day Twelve

Strategy: ABC Brainstorm

What to do (1–7 is the mini-lesson):

1. Gather students at the meeting area with their writer's notebooks.
2. On large chart paper, create an anchor chart titled "ABC Brainstorm for Ideas." The teacher explains the process of the ABC chart (to think of ideas to write on for each letter) as well as its purpose (to generate ideas for writing) and names it (ABC Brainstorm).
3. Read the book. Discuss genre, the author's purpose, time focus, connections, and information about the author's life.
4. Teacher adds his or her thoughts and ideas to the anchor chart (Think Aloud).

5. Students create an ABC chart in the **back** of their notebooks to resemble the anchor chart.
6. Students add to the ABC chart they have created. I am hoping the mentor text has helped generate some ideas for their ABC chart.
7. A couple of students share from their notebooks, and the teacher adds to the anchor chart.
8. Students write independently in the **front** of their notebooks for a set amount of time.
9. Students share. If a student has taken an idea from the day's mini-lesson and elaborated further on it, I let that student share first to help emphasize the strategy.

## Book: *Shortcut*, by Donald Crews

### Day Thirteen

Strategy: Listing with Emotions

What to do (1–7 is the mini-lesson):

1. Gather students at the meeting area with their writer's notebooks.
2. On large chart paper, create an anchor chart titled "A Time of Danger." The teacher explains the process of this strategy (to add emotion words to a basic list) as well as its purpose (to generate ideas and the emotions they brought about for writing) and names it (Listing with Emotions).
3. Read the book. Discuss genre, the author's purpose, time focus, connections, and information on the author's life.
4. Teacher adds his or her thoughts and ideas to the anchor chart (Think Aloud).
5. Students create a list in the **back** of their notebooks to resemble the anchor chart.
6. Students add to the list they have created. I am hoping the mentor text has helped generate some ideas for their list.
7. A couple of students share from their notebooks, and the teacher adds to the anchor chart.
8. Students write independently in the **front** of their notebooks for a set amount of time.
9. Students share. If a student has taken an idea from the day's mini-lesson and elaborated further on it, I let that student share first to help emphasize the strategy).

A student sample for this lesson is shown in Figure 4.16 (page 88).

**Figure 4.16**   Student Sample for Day Thirteen of Collecting

| | |
|---|---|
| | A Time of Danger |
| • | Driving my four wheeler |
| • | Swimming in Gulf of Mexico |
| • | Near the road |
| • | Bungy jumping |
| • | Flying in a airplane |
| • | Near some stray dogs |
| • | On a rollercoaster |
| • | Holding a knife |
| • | Near someone drunk or on drugs |
| • | At a shooting range |
| • | In the woods |
| • | Near a prison |
| • | Falling off a cliff |
| • | In a old old house |
| • | Near a lake full of gators in it |
| • | In a fight |
| • | Near bullies |
| • | Getting shot |
| • | In the zoo |
| • | Near a bad person |

## Book: *Tornado!* by Betsy Byers

### Day Fourteen
Strategy: Quick Write: Reacting to World

Reminders: chart for notebook (glue in notebooks before mini-lesson)

What to do (1–7 is the mini-lesson):

1. Gather students at the meeting area with their writer's notebooks.
2. On large chart paper, create an anchor chart titled "Quick Write: Reacting to World." The teacher explains the process of the strategy as well as its purpose (to allow your thoughts to flow without interruption) and names it (a Quick Write).
3. Read the book. Discuss genre, the author's purpose, time focus, connections, and information about the author's life.
4. Teacher adds his or her thoughts and ideas to the anchor chart (Think Aloud).
5. Students create a page in the **back** of their notebooks to resemble the anchor chart.
6. Students add to the page in their notebooks they have created. I am hoping the mentor text has helped generate some ideas for their Quick Write page.
7. A couple of students share from their notebooks, and the teacher adds to the anchor chart.
8. Students write independently in the **front** of their notebooks for a set amount of time.
9. Students share. If a student has taken an idea from the day's mini-lesson and elaborated further on it, I let that student share first to help emphasize the strategy.

## Additional Collecting Lessons for Expository Essays

### Book: *The Tiny Seed*, by Eric Carle

#### Day Two
Strategy: Webbing

What to do (1–7 is the mini-lesson):

1. Gather students at the meeting area with their writer's notebooks.
2. On chart paper, create an anchor chart titled "Transitions." The teacher explains the purpose of the strategy (to learn a variety of transitions) and names the strategy (Webbing).
3. Read the book, pointing out the transitions.

4. Teacher adds his or her thoughts and ideas to the anchor chart (Think Aloud).

5. Students create a chart in the **back** of their notebooks to resemble the anchor chart.

6. Students add to the chart they have created. I am hoping my examples and the mentor text have helped generate some ideas and examples for their own chart.

7. A couple of students share from their notebooks what the group has added to their charts so far.

8. Students continue to add examples of transitions.

9. When the students feel their chart is full of helpful examples, they may continue writing in the **front** of their notebooks as usual.

10. Students share. If a student has taken an idea from the day's mini-lesson and elaborated further on it, I let that student share first to help emphasize the strategy.

A student sample for this lesson is shown in Figure 4.17 (page 91).

## Book: *Birds*, by Caroline Arnold

### Day Three

Strategy: T-chart

What to do (1–7 is the mini-lesson):

1. Gather students at the meeting area with their writer's notebooks.

2. On chart paper, create an anchor T-chart titled "What I'm Good At/What I Know About." The teacher explains the purpose of the strategy (to generate ideas) and names the strategy (T-chart).

3. Read excerpts from the book.

4. Teacher adds to his or her thoughts and ideas to the anchor chart (Think Aloud).

5. Students create a T-chart in the **back** of their notebooks to resemble the anchor chart.

6. Students add to the chart they have created. I am hoping my examples and the mentor text have helped generate some ideas and examples for their own chart.

7. A couple of students share from their notebooks what they have added to their chart so far.

8. Students continue to add examples to their charts.

9. When the students feel their chart is full of helpful ideas, they may continue writing in the **front** of their notebooks as usual.

**Figure 4.17**  Student Sample for Day Two of Collecting

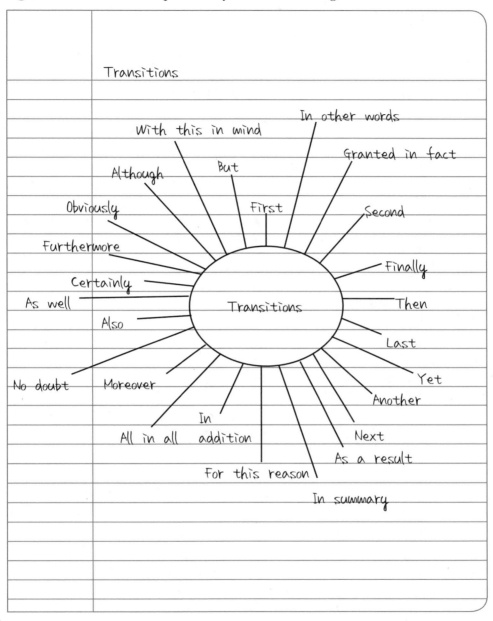

Transitions

Transitions

In other words
With this in mind
Granted in fact
Although
But
Obviously
First
Second
Furthermore
Finally
Certainly
Then
As well
Also
Last
No doubt
Moreover
Yet
Another
In
addition
All in all
Next
As a result
For this reason
In summary

10. Students share. If a student has taken an idea from the day's mini-lesson and elaborated further on it, I let that student share first to help emphasize the strategy.

A student sample for this lesson is shown in Figure 4.18 (page 93).

## Book: *Amelia to Zora*, by Cynthia Chin-Lee

### Day Four

Strategy: Webbing

What to do (1–7 is the mini-lesson):

1. Gather students at the meeting area with their writer's notebooks.
2. On chart paper, create an anchor chart titled "Important People." The teacher explains the purpose of the strategy (to generate ideas and details) and names the strategy (Webbing).
3. Read excerpts from the book.
4. Teacher adds his or her thoughts and ideas the the anchor chart (Think Aloud).
5. Students create a web in the **back** of their notebooks to resemble the anchor chart.
6. Students add to the web they have created. I am hoping my examples and the mentor text have helped generate some examples for their own web.
7. A couple of students share from their notebooks what they have added to their web so far.
8. Students continue to add examples to their charts.
9. When the students feel their web is full of helpful details, they may continue writing in the **front** of their notebooks as usual.
10. Students share. If a student has taken an idea from the day's mini-lesson and elaborated further on it, I let that student share first to help emphasize the strategy.

## Book: *Color for Thought*, by Fifth Graders at Coastal Episcopal School

### Day Five

Strategy: Listing

What to do (1–5 is the mini-lesson):

1. Gather students at the meeting area with their writer's notebooks.
2. On chart paper, create an anchor chart titled "Juicy Color Words." The teacher explains the purpose of the strategy (to

**Figure 4.18**   Student Sample for Day Three of Collecting

| What I'm good at | What I know about |
|---|---|
| Basketball | Math |
| Reading books | Writing |
| Drawing | Science |
| Video games | Multiplication |
| Homework | Plants |
| Fixing/building | Social studies |
| Getting good grades | My family |
| Helping my dad | Firefly and their lights |
| Sharing | How air bags work |
| Helping others | Subtraction |
| Solving strategies | Addition |
| School work | Division |
| Subtracting | Using compasses |
| Adding | Finding my direction with |
| Dividing | a map |
| Clue finding | The human ear |
| Planting | Gears/how they work |
| Counting money | Pullies |
| Working with others | |
| Helping my mom cook | |
| Cleaning my room | |

generate synonyms for basic color words) and names the strategy (Listing).

3. Students create a chart in the **back** of their notebooks to resemble the anchor chart.

4. Read each page of the book and stop after each one, so that students can collect color words in their notebooks.

5. Teacher asks for students to give examples from their notebooks and adds these to the anchor chart. (Think Aloud)

6. Students continue to add details and thoughts to their own charts.

7. When the students feel their chart is full of helpful color words, they may continue writing in the **front** of their notebooks as usual.

8. Students share. If a student has taken an idea from the day's mini-lesson and elaborated further on it, I let them share first to help emphasize the strategy.

I like to use the poem "The Garden," by Shel Silverstein, to enhance the lesson. This poem is filled with synonyms for basic color words. A student sample for this lesson is shown in Figure 4.19 (page 95).

## Book: *Mosquito Bite*, by Alexandra Siy

**Day Six**

Strategy: T-chart

Reminders: example from the book for student use (p. 18–19), overhead of a page from the book (pp. 3, 5, 6, 7)

What to do (1–7 is the mini-lesson):

1. Gather students at the meeting area with their writer's notebooks.

2. On chart paper, create an anchor chart titled "Interesting Facts/Beautiful Language." The teacher explains the purpose of the strategy (to generate ideas and details) and names the strategy (T-chart).

3. Read excerpts from the book. Model for students how to code a page from the book.

4. Teacher adds his or her thoughts and ideas to the anchor chart (Think Aloud).

5. Students create a T-chart in the **back** of their notebooks to resemble the anchor chart.

6. Students will code a page from the text. They will highlight interesting facts blue and beautiful language red. I am

**Figure 4.19** Student Sample for Day Five of Collecting

(Note that the student's errors have been retained for authenticity.)

|  | Juicy color words | |
|---|---|---|
|  | • Rasberry red | • Creme white |
|  | • Baby blue | • Blush red |
|  | • Night sky black | • Rouge red |
|  | • Highlighter yellow | • Paprika red |
|  | • Grass green | • Robins egg blue |
|  | • Lamb fur white | • Aquamarine blue |
|  | • Grass green | • Cornsilk yellow |
|  | • Tree bark brown | • Drab green |
|  | • Goldenrod orange | • Day glow orange |
|  | • Periwinkle purple | • Saffron orange |
|  | • Cocoa brown | • Hyacinth purple |
|  | • Cinnamon red | • Bruise pruple |
|  | • Marigold yellow | • Blood red |
|  | • Forest green | • Aubergine purple |
|  | • Midnight blue | • Sienna brown |
|  | • khaki green | • Terra-cotta brown |
|  | • Fluorescent orange | • Jet black |
|  | • Eggplant purple | • Ebony black |
|  | • Earthen brown | • Licorice black |
|  | • Soot black | • Chalky white |
|  | • Alabaster white | • Bleached white |
|  | • Sapphire red | • Firey gold |
|  | • Pearl pink | • Metal silver |

hoping my text examples will guide the students to code independently.

7. A couple of students share from their notebooks what they have added to their T-charts so far.

8. Students continue to add examples to their T-charts.

9. When the students feel their T-chart is full of helpful details, they may continue writing in the **front** of their notebooks as usual.

10. Students share. If a student has taken an idea from the day's mini lesson and elaborated further on it, I let that student share first to help emphasize the strategy.

## Book: *Oil Spill!* by Melvin Berger

### Day Seven

Strategy: Timeline

What to do (1–8 is the mini-lesson):

1. Gather students at the meeting area with their writer's notebooks.

2. On chart paper, create an anchor chart titled "Timeline Events." The teacher explains the purpose of the strategy (to put events in order) and names the strategy (timeline).

3. Read excerpts from the book (pages 1–13).

4. Teacher adds his or her thoughts and ideas to the anchor chart (Think Aloud).

5. Students create a timeline in the **back** of their notebooks to resemble the anchor chart.

6. Students add to the timeline, with the teacher's guidance, major events of the story.

7. Now students create a new timeline in which major events from their own life will be added. I am hoping my examples and the mentor text have helped generate some examples for their own personal timeline.

8. A couple of students will share what they have added to their personal timeline so far.

9. Students continue to add events to their timeline.

10. When the students feel their timeline is full of helpful details, they may continue writing in the **front** of their notebooks as usual.

11. Students share. If a student has taken an idea from the day's mini-lesson and elaborated further on it, I let that student share first to help emphasize the strategy.

## Book: *Welcome to the Green House*, by Jane Yolen

### Day Eight
Strategy: Listing (Onomatopoeia)
What to do (1–7 is the mini-lesson):
1. Gather students at the meeting area with their writer's notebooks.
2. On chart paper, create an anchor chart titled "Onomato-poeia." The teacher explains the purpose of the strategy (to generate examples for onomatopoeia) and names the strategy (listing).
3. Read excerpts from book.
4. Teacher adds his or her thoughts and ideas to the anchor chart (Think Aloud).
5. Students create a list in the **back** of their notebooks to resemble the anchor chart.
6. Students add to the list they have created. I am hoping my examples and the mentor text have helped generate some examples for their own list.
7. A couple of students share from their notebooks what they have added to their list so far.
8. Students continue to add examples to their charts.
9. When the students feel their chart is full of helpful details, they may continue writing in the **front** of their notebooks as usual.
10. Students share. If a student has taken an idea from the day's mini-lesson and elaborated further on it, I let that student share first to help emphasize the strategy.

## Book: *A Day in the Prairie*, by Kildeer Countryside Elementary School

### Day Nine
Strategy: T-chart (Sense/Describing Detail)
What to do (1–7 is the mini-lesson):
1. Gather students at the meeting area with their writer's notebooks.
2. On chart paper, create an anchor T-chart titled "Sense/ Describing Detail." The teacher explains the purpose of the strategy (to generate ideas and details for a topic) and names the strategy (T-chart).
3. Read the book.

4. Teacher adds his or her thoughts and ideas to the anchor chart (Think Aloud).
5. Students create a chart in the **back** of their notebooks to resemble the anchor chart.
6. Students add to the T-chart they have created. I am hoping my examples and the mentor text has helped generate some ideas and details for their own chart.
7. A couple of students share from their notebooks what they have added to their chart so far.
8. Students continue to add details and thoughts to their charts.
9. When the students feel their chart is full of helpful details, they may continue writing in the **front** of their notebooks as usual.
10. Students share. If a student has taken an idea from the day's mini-lesson and elaborated further on it, I let that students share first to help emphasize the strategy.

*Chapter Five*

# Marinating

"Writing a story is like going down a path in the woods. You don't worry about getting lost, you just go."

—Jan Brett

## Marinating: The Bridge to Drafting

Recently I conducted a writing workshop, and as I began to elaborate on the "marinating" step of the process I admit I received a couple of unusual glances from the crowd. I laughingly told them, "No, I am not talking filet mignon, rather reflection and planning."

To put it simply, a writer marinates by "going back to the moment" when working on a narrative or memoir. It can also mean research, especially if students are working on an informational piece, like an expository essay.

So why do I call it marinating? Because to me it implies a soaking of information and thoughts, not a quick dash sprinkled here and there. I am a writer, and because of this, I know that in order to hone in on details and remember the moments as if they were yesterday, I need to take time to recall. What could be a problem with this? Time. Do we ever have enough of it? No, and in our classrooms we feel the time crunch now more than ever. However, I have found that if I give my students time to marinate on their self-selected ideas or topics, the writing is filled with passion and voice and those details for which teachers are constantly begging. So, in essence, I am saving time. I believe that if we are continuously asking our students to add details, maybe the problem is not so much the lack of details as the lack of time—time needed to think through and plan and gather and collect . . . and, yes, marinate. So how does this save time? If I slow down a little and approach each stage of the process as a stroll rather than as a sprint, the foundation I am laying for my students is solid, and I do not have to repeat myself or reteach many of my lessons. I find that marinating paves the road to drafting and adds a comfort for the students, a comfort that they will be successful in their writing. Writer Ken Follett says it perfectly: "Everything is planned.

I spend a long time outlining. It's the only way I know to get all the ducks in a row. . . . The research is the easiest. The outline is the most fun because you can do anything." I simply tell my students that we marinate to remember, research, plan, and get our ducks all in a row.

## Exactly How Do Students Marinate?

There are certain strategies I like to teach my students. These strategies can be used to collect, marinate, and revise. I am not sure I could teach writing without them. I teach my students the importance of these strategies, no matter what genre of writing they are working on. Here are those strategies and the stages in which they are used. These same strategies were seen in the collecting lessons in Chapter Four.

- Webbing (collecting, marinating, revising)
- T-charts (collecting, marinating, revising)
- Quick sketches (collecting and marinating)
- Timelines (collecting and marinating)
- Column charts (collecting, marinating, revising)
- Writing back (collecting)
- Listing (collecting and marinating)

These strategies are the core of our writing workshop. To me, the test of a strategy's effectiveness is whether it can be used again and again in many facets of writing. Lessons, however, can only be used once. So my goal as a writing teacher is to lay the foundation of the process with strategies and use purposeful lessons to introduce and elaborate on these strategies.

Let me take you on a conversational journey that shows how two students used these strategies to marinate on their writing. You will find Alex's actual marinating samples in Figures 5.1 and 5.2 (pages 101 and 102).

**Me:** Alex, I am so intrigued by your idea to write about your Newfoundland trip. I can't wait to read it. Where are you right now in the process?

**Alex:** I am marinating with a list. I am trying to list as many facts and events as I can remember. This trip occurred several years ago, so I want to try and remember it all. Well, as much as I can.

**Me:** That is an excellent idea. You know me. I am "the girl of a hundred lists." I will check back tomorrow and see how it is going.

**Figure 5.1** Marinating Sample with a List of Facts

(Note that the student's errors have been retained for authenticity.)

| | |
|---|---|
| | Newfoundland Facts |
| • | Puffin is provincial bird |
| • | Iceburgs take 10,000 years to form in Greenland before they break off and go to Newfoundland |
| • | When it is foggy, you can hear the fog horn |
| • | Humpback whales are seen between May and September |
| • | The Titanic sunk off the coast of Newfoundland in 1912 |
| • | On the flag, white means snow and ice, blue means sea, red means |

**Figure 5.2** Marinating Sample with a Timeline

(Note that the student's errors have been retained for authenticity.)

Trip to Newfoundland, Canada

Timeline

5 — We had to go home. I was so mad because I wanted to stay

4 — I went to Signal Hill to see the place where soldiers watched for people invading. I got a stuffed puffin there.

3 — Later, I got to have fish and chips for the first time, it was so good!

2 — After we got there, we went on a boat tour to see iceburgs & puffins

1 — We went to a bunch of airports

**Me:** How's it going, Alex? Did you finish your list from yesterday? May I see it?

**Alex:** I sure did. I am surprised at how many informational facts I remembered. Even though this is a personal narrative, you always tell us to sprinkle in background information to help the reader. Today I am starting to marinate in a different way. I am creating a timeline of events.

**Me:** What a great job on this list of facts. I like how you are also using a timeline. It helps writers keep everything in sequential order. I also appreciate how you continued with the way we used a timeline in class. You used one side for "chunks of time" and the other for "details." You are doing a great job.

**Alex:** Thanks. I believe I will be ready to draft tomorrow. The story is really coming back to me while I am marinating.

**Me:** That's wonderful. I look forward to seeing what you will do this piece. I know it will be great.

Now let's go to another student, Leah. She is also at the marinating stage of the process. Her samples are shown in Figures 5.3 and 5.4 (pages 104 and 105).

**Me:** Hey, Leah, how's it going?

**Leah:** Great! I just started to marinate with a web. I am writing about going to Grandma's house.

**Me:** Wonderful. Now, let me ask, why did you choose a web to marinate?

**Leah:** I like the web because it helps me empty my brain of events and details. After I finish my web, I like to go back, like you showed us, and figure out which details go at the beginning, middle, or end of me story. It helps me "see" my story.

**Me:** I could not have said that better myself. This type of "storm and sort" really helps the writer hone in on the important events. I can see you started this web and you already have a good bit of information on there. It sounds like you enjoy going to Grandma's house. I will check back tomorrow and see where you are at in the process.

*The Next Day*

**Me:** Good morning, Leah. So, how's it going with that web?

**Leah:** I finished the web yesterday, and today I am working on a quick sketch. I like to marinate with that strategy.

**Me:** A quick sketch is an excellent choice. Why did you choose it?

**Figure 5.3** Marinating Sample with a Quick Sketch

(Note that the student's errors have been retained for authenticity.)

**Figure 5.4**   Marinating Sample with a $W_5 + H_1$ Web

(Note that the student's errors have been retained for authenticity.)

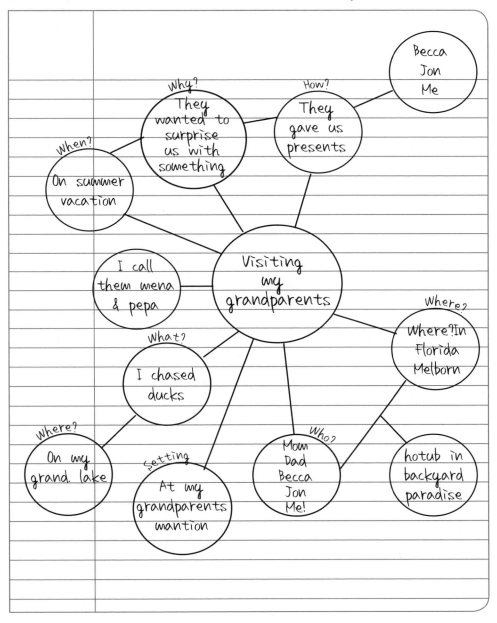

I would like to share a quote that I use to show my students that "real writers" create quick sketches:

*"Try drawing or painting a scene you're working on. Often this will help free up your imagination."* —Kevin Henkes

**Leah:** Well, I am working on trying to put more setting in my story, and I think if I do a quick sketch of Grandma's farm and house, it will be easier for me to add those details to my story.

**Me:** That is my favorite way to use a quick sketch. I like to use it for settings and characters. You know, starting your story off with a setting is a powerful technique writers use. Remember how Patricia Polacco started her book *Thunder Cake* with a setting? It made us feel like we were there. This quick sketch may be just what you need. Good job, Leah. Have you thought about how you are going to sort that information in your web?

**Leah:** I feel comfortable labeling the web with the W5 + H1 method, so I will use that. I think this quick sketch will help me recall details, not just for the setting but for the labeling as well. I really wanted to "see" the farm again before I began to sort my information.

**Me:** You are thinking like a writer, Leah. I look forward to seeing that quick sketch and your labeling web as well.

Leah isn't feeling any pressure of time or that a certain order must take place during her marinating. Some students like to brainstorm one day and immediately sort the information the next. Not Leah, at least not this time. She chose to break it up a little and work on a quick sketch in between the "storm and sort." This plan sounded good to me. She is becoming an independent writer and an independent thinker.

Donald Graves has said that "90 percent of the writing process takes place before the draft." And once I started allowing my students more time to reflect and research, the more I realized how true this statement is.

## Another Reason to Marinate

Because I know that the writing process is recursive, I understand the importance of marinating. Sometimes, even after careful thought, a student will select an idea that is just not going anywhere. The stage of marinating often catches this before drafting takes place, which is important. Let me give you a concrete example.

Last year, after collecting and selecting, a student of mine named Brady was ready to marinate. The method of storm and sort was a favorite of his, so this is what he chose. "Storm and sort" simply means that students brainstorm details about an idea or topic they have selected. They can brainstorm with a web or a list. I have taught my students that it is important to sort this information in order to see where more details may be needed. It might be the ending of a narrative or the first point paragraph in an expository. Brady was still in the "storming" part when he looked up at me and said, "Ms. Morris, I can't think of anything about this topic of whales I chose." I asked him if he needed a day of research to help him pump up his details. His response made me smile. "Actually, I have no passion about whales after all. I really don't think I want to go any further with this. May I change my topic to one of the others I chose and added to the sticky note?" I appreciated the honesty. And if I was a firm believer that all students should go through the writing process at the same time in sequential order, I would have made Brady stick to his topic with the thought that it may have taught him a valuable lesson. The only lesson I can think of that it would have taught would be you'd better get it right the first time or you're stuck.

In contrast, I build in two to three days to marinate for this exact reason. No one gets everything right the first time, and Brady learned more from realizing he needed to move on to something else than by taking a topic he wasn't ready to write about all the way through publication. By offering him time to plan and reflect and possibly research, I gave him a chance to test out his topic. If it stood the test of time through marinating, it is probably a topic that deserves to make it to publication. It's all about getting those ducks in a row.

Now, if you are concerned about how often changing topics or ideas happens, I can assure you, from my experience, it is not often. I also keep a pretty firm rule that once you start drafting, there is no going back. If I let students continue changing writing topics or ideas at any stage of the process, their chances of meeting the deadline would be slim. It is a give-and-take world in my classroom. I will give you the time to plan and test your topic or idea (aka marinate), and in return I expect the process to be taken seriously and hard work to be evident at every stage, and this includes marinating.

## A Note on Marinating

I love the writer's notebook, and so much of what we do is salvaged in there. These salvaged treasures include our marinating.

We marinate in the back of the notebook. Let's go back to Alex for a moment. Alex, after several days of marinating, has concrete examples of her work and her planning, examples she can refer to again and again, not just for this piece of writing but also for future pieces. If, during a conference, I see a student with bare-bones or minimum details, I can have them look back at other times they marinated and say, "See what a nice job you did here? Well, for this new piece of writing, I want to see your marinating just as thoughtful." It is a critical part of our process. It's all about allowing time.

## A Closer Look at the Strategies Used for Marinating

I would like to take a moment to go over just how we use those previously listed strategies in the marinating stage. Many of these will be apparent when you look through the student samples later in this chapter, but a more thorough explanation will ensure your confidence in teaching them and your students' confidence in using them. When my students marinate, I want them to plan and remember and collect details and moments that will bring the story or essay to life. The following strategies offer my students a place to house all the information going through their minds. They help students create a personal writing plan that will make the job of drafting less daunting.

### Webbing

One of the best ways I have found for my students to marinate is with the webbing strategy. It is the first step in our storm and sort method as discussed earlier. But there is more to a web than just that. Sometimes, while marinating, my students have a difficult time recalling events for the beginning (or middle or end) of a narrative. If they need to hone in on that one particular moment of their story, taking that certain event and inserting it into a web helps them focus on one moment at a time. Let's say I have a student who has decided to write a personal narrative on her camping trip with her family. She is now marinating (thinking back) and planning for this story. While marinating, she has no problem with remembering the beginning of the trip, but she seems to lose a little steam with regards to the details of the moment she saw a snake. So she simply puts the words "Moment I saw snake" in the middle of her web and tries to think about every detail she can about that one moment. What did the snake look like? Where was she when she saw the snake? How did she feel at that particular moment? If I can get her to focus on the snake moment, because that is where the action is in her story, which is what we refer to as the hover moment, she will be able to not only see it for herself but also help the reader see it.

For an expository piece, webbing may be used to remember facts and opinions based on a particular topic and research. For example, if a boy selected an expository topic about his favorite holiday and is now trying to organize his thoughts into three reasons he chose this holiday (Christmas, for example), he may use three webs, one for each major point (the smells, the presents, and decorations). Or he may find he is only struggling to think of details for just his second point, the presents. Then I would suggest he put presents in the center of a web and think about why this makes Christmas so special.

To me, a web can serve two functions. It can serve as a general tool for brainstorming or as a great specific tool to help students look at one moment in their stories or one point in their essays. A student sample of a web is shown in Figure 5.5 (page 110).

## T-chart

I couldn't teach without the T-chart. We use the T-chart to share, collect, marinate, and revise. Let me show you a couple of ways to use this tool for marinating. Remember that we marinate in order to go back to the moment we are writing about or to research and plan an expository. My students have found that one way to successfully use a T-chart is when attaching emotions to an event in a piece of writing they are working on. I have modeled for my students the process of putting a particular event from their writing on the left side of the T-chart and then brainstorming all of the emotions that were felt during that event. This chart is referred to an emotion/event T-chart. (See Figure 5.6 on page 111.) The exact same thing can be done for a character in the story, and it would be referred to as a character/emotion T-chart.

For an expository essay, the T-chart is used a little differently. Let's take an essay that deals mostly with explaining why. Let's look back at the student who selected the topic of a favorite holiday: Christmas. He can use a T-chart much like a web when thinking of details for each of his points. On the left side of the chart he would put the three topic points (smell, presents, and decorations), and on the right side of the chart he would list why the smell, presents, and

**Figure 5.5** A Narrative Marinating Sample Using a Web

(Note that the student's errors have been retained for authenticity.)

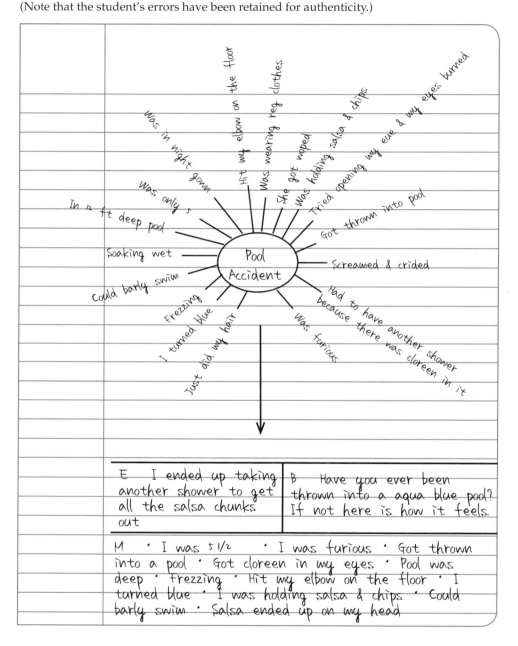

E  I ended up taking another shower to get all the salsa chunks out

B  Have you ever been thrown into a aqua blue pool? If not here is how it feels.

M  • I was 5 1/2  • I was furious • Got thrown into a pool • Got cloreen in my eyes • Pool was deep • frezzing • Hit my elbow on the floor • I turned blue • I was holding salsa & chips • Could barly swim • Salsa ended up on my head

**Figure 5.6**  Emotion/Event T-Chart

(Note that the student's errors have been retained for authenticity.)

| Emotion | Event |
|---------|-------|
| Lonely | No friends |
| Heroic | Saved lives |
| Accepted | He had friends |
| Happy | Talking to others |
| Synpothetic | Fish caught in net |
| Hopeless | He was trapped |
| Relieved | He was thrown back |
| Left out | No one plays with me |
| Loved | Mom and Dad loves on me |
| Helpful | Help some one |
| Forgiven | When I saved my friend from folling |

decorations are so important to him that Christmas is his favorite holiday. See his T-chart in Figure 5.7 (page 113).

Now let's look at how a boy researching a self-selected topic (animals) would use the T-chart. On the left side of the chart he would put the three animals he is studying, and on the right side of the chart he would record his research findings about each of those animals. See his T-chart in Figure 5.8 (page 114). The T-chart serves as a place to capture details from moments he has experienced or research he has conducted.

## Quick Sketch

As I noted earlier, when my student Leah wanted to remember more about the setting of her grandmother's farm, she used a quick sketch. I teach my students that quick sketches must be accompanied by labels. It is important to label all the specific details the quick sketch conjured up. If Leah can remember all the little things about her grandmother's farm, like the fence in front of the apple tree and the cows grazing to the left of the barn, she is better prepared to help the reader see this wonderful setting because she can now see it for herself. Having something to look at made it a little easier for her to describe the details of the farm. This technique works great for a character description, too. I was writing a story for *Chicken Soup for the Soul* and I needed to make sure my readers could see my character: a chocolate Labrador retriever named Tootsie. I took a moment to draw Tootsie (and I am no artist; my sister received all of that talent in the family), but it helped me add details to her appearance. I was able, through the quick sketch, to label that she had a delightful girth, a muzzle speckled with gray, and the perfectly triangular ears that only Labs have. I saved this precious girl from a shelter, and I named her Tootsie because she was built, to me, like a Tootsie Roll. My students loved seeing my quirky drawing, and then when I shared the beginning paragraph about her funny appearance, it brought it all home for them. It grabbed their attention, and they wanted me to read more. That is the purpose of a quick sketch: to give the writer a visual and then help the writer show this visual to the reader. This strategy works great for a personal narrative, but it also works great for an expository.

Let's go back to the student researching animals. While researching, he may come across some illustrations of the animals he is writing about, and these illustrations show how each body part helps them survive. Because I have modeled for him the value of

**Figure 5.7**   Student Sample

(Note that the student's errors have been retained for authenticity.)

| | 3 Reasons | Why |
|---|---|---|
| | Christmas | |
| | 1. The smell | • It could make me think it's Christmas <br> • It could smell really sweet. <br> • It could be something good to eat.    • Juisy pies <br> • Yucky fruit cake <br> • Sweet smelling cinnamon candle |
| | 2. The presents | • It's fun to unwrap the presents. <br> • There could be something you really want.    • Wii <br> • Video game <br> • PS3 |
| | 3. The decorations | • They're really fun. <br> • You could play with them. <br> • You could decorate the decorations.    • Fuzzy streamers <br> • Deer statue <br> • Ball ordaments |

**Figure 5.8** Student Sample

(Note that the student's errors have been retained for authenticity.)

| Animal | Facts |
|---|---|
| Black Salamander | • 2 out of 10 eggs are able to develop.<br>• 4 to 5 inches long<br>• Gestation can last 3 years |
| Eagle Ray | • Male weights 26 pounds<br>• Small teeth called denticles cover the body<br>• Female weights 155 pounds<br>• They live in warm water and feed on oysters. crabs. and lobsters. |
| Basilisk | • Can run on water when it Is frightened<br>• 2 foot long reptile<br>• It is one of the most timid animals. |

the quick-sketch strategy, he chooses to gather this new information by creating his own quick sketch, labeling the specific body parts and how they play an important role in survival. Because he made a sketch, this valuable information stands a better chance of being remembered and put into his own words than if he had simply taken notes. This restating of information is one of our goals for expository essays. It is also important to note that most of my male students love to draw. It excites them to know they have the opportunity to do so in writing. In his wonderful book *Boy Writers*, Ralph Fletcher investigates why test scores are indicating that boys have fallen far behind girls in all grades in the area of writing. He explains how topic choice and the importance of drawing are crucial to the success of boy writers. Each chapter ends with a section titled "What can I do in my classroom?" That objective is my goal as well. I want my boys to love to write, and I must say that they do. I can't count the number of times parents have stopped me at the beginning of the year expressing concern that their son hates to write. My standard comment is "Just give me until October; he will be hooked." And he is. I feel this is in part to the fact that I not only allow them to write about what they want, but I allow them the time to do what boys love: research, share, and create quick sketches. It is a win-win situation.

## Timelines

Sequencing can be an issue for many young writers. They know what they want to say, but somehow in the process of writing it all down, the order of events gets jumbled and leaves the reader confused. Good writing is organized, and the timeline strategy helps my students achieve this. When my students are marinating for the first time, I like to introduce the timeline strategy. It quickly becomes a favorite for personal narratives. I ask my students to draw a basic timeline, and then I go a step further and explain that the left side of the timeline is for chunks of time and the right side is for details. I also let them know that our chunks of time are not that different from a basic storyboard, but that by putting this information on one side of the timeline, it saves the other side for adding details. I caution my students that starting off, they probably won't need more than five chunks of time: one for the beginning, three for the middle, and, of course, one for the ending. One of the sections used in the middle should be salvaged for the hover moment. Remember that the hover moment is the critical part of the plot where the action, emotion, and turning point take place. It amazes my students when I ask them to read their completed "chunks of time" side only. It sounds like a story, has a logical order, but is *bare bones*. Then, I ask for them to begin to add details to the right side, focusing on "one chunk at a time." When this is finished, I ask them to read the timeline again, considering both sides in the reading. My students begin to realize the absolute necessity of those details in making their story interesting.

I also remind my students that when they are thinking of details for each of their five areas plotted on the timeline, it is important to anticipate any questions the reader may have and answer those questions before the reader gets the chance to wonder. Remember my conversation with Alex? She created a timeline for her story about Newfoundland and it helped her keep the story sequentially organized. (See Figure 5.2, page 102.) This sequence was not only for her, but for her readers as well. Another sample timeline is shown in Figure 5.9 (page 117).

## Column Chart

The column-chart strategy is the twin of webbing. It is the place for organizing all of the information that has flooded the web. It is where my students sort their brainstorming. Earlier, I explained the storm-and-sort method, and I teach my students that the column chart is a great place to organize all of that information they just brainstormed, a place to sort it. At the beginning of each year, my students come to me as webbing kings and queens. It is obviously a favorite way many teachers teach students to brainstorm. The problem, I have found, with only using a web to brainstorm is that when my students start to draft, one of two things happens: Either my students don't refer back to the web again or the scattered information on the web confuses them, so they don't have the opportunity to focus on the parts of their writing that may be lacking details. If my students use only the web strategy and do not take the time to do something with that information, it gets lost in the writing. A web isn't organized and it's not supposed to be, but good writing is. A column chart ensures that the brainstorming gets organized. I equate it to a grocery list. If I webbed my grocery list and then took off to shop, I would find myself all over the store and would probably leave without everything I needed. If I web what I need to buy and then use a column chart to organize the items based on where they are in the store (produce/frozen/dairy), I have created an efficient and more organized way to shop.

**Figure 5.9**  Timeline of Events Sample

(Note that the student's errors have been retained for authenticity.)

| | |
|---|---|
| | Enberrising moment (Timeline) |
| Track was made of 5 tall hills that consist only of dirt or clay. Many people come to ride bikes. skate park for people who ride bikes. skateboards. or use rollerblades. | Riding bikes in Fort Walton. Cloud day. Christmas Eve. Tempurture just right. Got tired. Needed to rest. Drank some gaterade. Wanted to watch people |
| Tower tall enough to see the entier area even the park and the soccer field right next to it. Don't use stairs to get to the top. | ride there bikes from the wooden tower. Climb to the top. People riding to what seemed to me the pseed of light. |
| You use stairs to get up and down and can slide down on it. | Wanted to ride again. Slid down off the wooden tower and ripped my |
| Riders really fast. Track holds bike races. | pants. Didn't realize I did. |
| What would be funnyer than a 7 yr old boy ripping his pants. | Dad tells me I ripped my pants. Also noticed I got a splinter had to go home. |
| Really embarrist. And it was Christmas Eve! | |

Let's look at a student who is working on a personal narrative. She is in the stage of marinating, and here is our conversation:

**Me:** How's it going, Haley? I see you completed your web yesterday. You have so many details and events on that web. I love it. Explain what your plans for today are.

**Haley:** Well, I almost think I have too much information. I want to sort this information in the B/M/E column chart and find out what I need more or less of.

**Me:** Excellent. May I sit here and watch you for a moment?

**Haley:** Of course you can (she gives me a big smile).

As I sat there observing, I noted how Haley drew the three columns on a page in the back of her writer's notebook. She labeled the first column with a *B* for the beginning. The second column she labeled with an *M* for the middle, and the last column she labeled with an *E* for the ending. At this point, she began to reread her web. As she read what she had written on the web, she sorted the information to the B/M/E column chart depending on where that detail or event fit. She did this for as many of the items she brainstormed as she felt were important. This took approximately seven minutes, and then she appeared finished. I would not normally sit with a student for this whole process. Instead, I circulate to others and then come back. But I wanted to see how and what she was thinking. This is metacognition at its best.

**Me:** OK, Haley, what have you inferred from the storm-and-sort process you just completed?

**Haley:** I realize I have so many details and events that go in the beginning and ending of my story. I am afraid my middle isn't "so mighty" after all.

**Me:** What do you think you need to do about this?

**Haley:** I need to go back and try to remember those major events and details that happened in the middle. The middle is the heart of the story. It is where all the action takes place. And most of my action is found at the beginning.

**Me:** That is an excellent observation. After reading your web, I can see you have a good bit of information added to it. Instead of simply adding more to your web to try and pump up the middle of your story, what else could you do?

**Haley:** You know, I could also rethink some of those events I have put in the beginning. Maybe some of those really fit better in the middle of my story after all.

**Me:** I think you are on the right track and thinking like a writer. Remember, we need the first three seconds to grab our reader, but we must sustain their interest with the rising and falling action that occurs in the middle. And never forget the hover moment . . . that moment when things began to change in the story that is so important. We don't want a flat story, now do we?

**Haley:** (Laughing) Thanks, I think I will use tomorrow to look a little closer at what I have. It isn't that I don't necessarily have enough; it might just be misplaced a little.

The column chart is also a beneficial strategy for an expository essay. Let's go back to the student who wanted to write about animals. His favorite animal is a shark, and other than the Labrador retriever, that is also my favorite. We connected because of our mutual interest. My students know what I like to write about and I know the same about them. It is all for the good of our community of writers. So for this scenario, I recount a little bit of our conference and how the column chart and the quick sketch helped him create an informative plan that ultimately led him to publishing success with this piece of writing.

**Me:** How's it going, Bill? I see a fine web of great white shark facts in front of you. . . . I love it. What are your plans for today?

**Bill:** Well, I did a good bit of research yesterday. I emptied my brain of all I could remember about the great white, and I realized I needed some more information, so I read a couple of your shark books from the "Ocean Animals" basket. Then I added that information to the web. Today I am going to sort the details and facts in this web into a column chart.

**Me:** Sounds like a plan to me. How do you plan on sorting that information? Into what three areas are you going to divide all the facts and details you have on your web? Our expository essays typically have the three points we are explaining to the reader.

**Bill:** At this point, I am not sure. I am hoping that part will come as I begin to reread what all I have in this web.

**Me:** Do you mind if I sit here awhile and watch you sort this information?

**Bill:** That's fine.

As with Haley, I am going to let you see what I was seeing. Bill began to reread, and I noticed him putting stars beside some details and some facts. Then I noticed he was putting bullets by other entries in his web. It always amazes me to watch my students sort their information. Out of the 96 students I teach writing to each day, I believe there are days I see 96 different ways of thinking. Truly amazing.

Next, I watched as Bill drew his three-column chart in the back of his notebook. He put a star as the label for the first column. Then he put a bullet as the label for the second column, and then he hesitated. I assumed he was trying to think of a symbol for his third point. After a second or two, he added an asterisk to the third column. Then he went back to his web and coded the information he had in that web to correlate with the three symbols he had chosen for his column chart.

At this point he began to transfer that information. After just a few minutes, he looked up at me and smiled.

**Me:** You look pleased. What did you just discover?

**Bill:** I found a good bit of information and discovered that my three points are going to be:

1. *What* the great white eats (these were his "starred" details and facts)

2. *Where* the great white can be found (these were his "bulleted" details and facts)

3. *Why* the great white is referred to as the perfect predator (these were his "asterisked" details and facts)

**Me:** That sounds like a great plan. I like how you honed in on "what, where, and why." That is important when explaining to your readers. Tell me a little more about your third point: "Why the great white is a perfect predator."

**Bill:** The way the great white is built, from its teeth to its tail, is perfect for hunting.

**Me:** Can you think of one of our marinating strategies that might really help you show the reader this third point?

**Bill:** (With a huge smile on his face) That would be the quick sketch, Ms. Morris. And I love drawing, especially great white sharks.

**Me:** Great minds think alike. I can definitely see how drawing major parts of the great white in a quick sketch will help you help your readers see how amazing these animals are, and, well, how they are "perfect predators."

**Bill:** I was actually thinking that would be a great title for my essay: "The Great White: A Perfect Predator."

**Me:** I love it. I can't wait to read your essay. I will check back with you tomorrow and see how that quick sketch is going. Good job, Bill.

Don't you love when things work out as perfectly as they did for Bill? His excitement was contagious. He webbed and, had I not shown him how to sort that information into a column chart, I am afraid all of that information he had collected would have been a little overwhelming to him when it came time to draft. Remember, he wasn't even sure what his three points were before he began to sort the information in a column chart. This strategy, when paired with a web, is magical for many students. But some students aren't fans of the web, and so I show them how to brainstorm with a list. A student's brainstorming list is shown in Figure 5.10 (page 122).

### Listing

I am an organized thinker. Well, I like to think I am! Actually, I am as ADHD as many of my students, and because of this personality trait, a web can sometimes be a little distracting for me. The whole "circular thing" can cause havoc with my thinking processes and the organization of the material. I share this information with my students. We know each other this intimately. It's what builds our community of trust and acceptance. I also let them know that they may choose to *list* the information that would typically go in a web. It may be easier for them to absorb all of the details, events, and facts. The web and the list are basically the same thing, but they are differentiated based on the needs, comfort levels, or desires of my students. See Figure 5.11 (page 123) for an example of how a student used a list that functions like a web.

## A Final Thought

Once my students learn who they are as writers, they certainly don't need me to tell them how they have to marinate. It is my job to show them several strategies, and how these strategies can help them plan out their essays and stories. It is up to the students to choose the strategies that fit their personalities and learning styles. Remember that marinating is the bridge to successful drafting. A good plan is a good start that gives our students a better chance at a good draft—one that will make its way successfully through the journey to publication.

Marinating, in my particular case, has proven to be an essential step in the writing process. It is so much more than just planning.

**Figure 5.10** Marinating Sample Using a B, M, E List

(Note that the student's errors have been retained for authenticity.)

| | |
|---|---|
| | Marinating B. M. E |
| | • I was six years old. |
| | • Got a new skateboard from Walmart. |
| B | • Rode it with Lea (My sister) outside. |
| | • Lea rode on a blue and black scooter. She did cool 360 |
| | • I went down a hill to show off my move. |
| | • Started out Good. Everything went wrong. |
| M | • I lost balance and started falling. |
| a | • Triped then got hit by skateboard. |
| g | • Lea raced after me while I was falling. |
| n | • I got hit in the face by the road. |
| i | • I got a very, very, very bloody nose. |
| f | • Fell six feet down and landed on my back. |
| i | • Lea went down the hill and jumped the sixfeet gap. |
| c | • My sister picked me up and carried me home. |
| e | • I passed out before I got home. |
| n | • She carried me on two blocks. |
| t | • I had scratches all over my legs and elbows. |
| | • Got to the house and my mom put a wet cloth on |
| M | my nose and wiped the blood off. |
| | • I woke up and my sister was right there with me. |
| E | • I had patches all over my legs and arms covering up the scratches. |
| | • She helped me up and put me over on the couch to turn on a movie. |
| | • I learned not to be a show-off. |
| | |
| | |
| | |
| | |

**Figure 5.11** Marinating Sample Using a List and a Web

(Note that the student's errors have been retained for authenticity.)

Pets

- Different kinds of pets
- Pets are popular and the only animals that people or owners keep
- Most well known pets are dogs and sometimes cats
- Pets can be dangerous or safe.
- Pets can have different characteristics like hard shells. floppy ears. spots. long hair. short hair. feathers. slimy. or soft
- Pets need daily exercise
- Pets have to eat and drink
- Pets are very suspicious and mischeifious
- Chocolate is very paisinous

Fetch

Walk — Caring for pets

Everyday

Feed them

Water

Caring for pets

Cleaning (Bathe)

It is thinking and rethinking and organizing information as well as having time for reflecting back on events and facts. It is about learning who we are as writers, both my students and myself. Marinating is the stroll, not sprint, to the next step of the process: drafting.

## Chapter Six

# Drafting and Sharing

"The beautiful part about writing is that you don't have to get it right the first time, unlike, say, a brain surgeon."

—Robert Cormier

## We Are Ready to Draft

Drafting isn't a test. It is a chance to free the story we have selected and marinated on. It is that first step of commitment to a piece of writing, and even though it is a critical step, it is one that should not be taken full of fear and doubt. It is the first step of many more to come. Many students feel blinded by the brightness of a blank page, and it is our job, as teachers of writing, to prepare them for the task at hand. As Phyllis Reynolds Naylor (author of *Shiloh*) says, "The first draft is a skeleton—just bare bones. It's like the very first rehearsal of a play, where the director moves the actors around mechanically to get a feel of the action."

## Step One: The Down Draft

Once my students have spent two or three days marinating, it is time to draft. We close our notebooks, gather our supplies, and let the next step begin. We keep our drafting supply list pretty simple: pencils without erasers and yellow legal-sized paper.

As with any stage of the process, there are steps within the stage. Drafting is no different. We call the first step the "down draft," in which our goal is simply to get the story down. As I stated earlier, our writer's notebooks are closed during this step. Donald M. Murray, in his 2004 book, *A Writer Teaches Writing*, confirms why this is so important. "The writer should put aside

125

all notes while writing a first draft. What is remembered is usually what should be remembered, and what is forgotten is usually what should be left out." If you have not had the opportunity to read *A Writer Teaches Writing*, I would urge you to do so. This insightful book has helped me, like no other book to date, on the fundamentals of writing and revising. I believe I am Donald M. Murray's biggest fan.

The act of pushing aside the notebook is important for all types of writing, but I find it critical with expository writing. It has been my experience that students rely too heavily on their research notes and end up simply "word moving" the facts around instead of putting them in their own words. This is not what teachers want. We want authentic research and original construction of the essays with splashes of cited information here and there. If all that students do is recopy the facts they found word-for-word, then, in truth, the writers who wrote the informational articles wrote their essays.

As for narrative pieces of writing, students can become too dependent on their planning and worry more about trying to copy details from the plan instead of simply writing a story. This over-reflecting on a plan can cause the draft to become burdened with unnecessary details and slow down the process of the down draft. After two or three days marinating on a personal narrative idea, the students have been provided the time necessary to go back to the moment.

I explain my expectations to my students and then ask them to close their notebooks and let them know that the information in the notebooks will be revisited again soon. A draft shouldn't be an inflated version of research or a plan. It is tiny fragments of what is interesting. It is my job to show my students how to resist the urge to see these outlines and plans as more valuable than the draft. Because I have taken the time to discuss the purpose of this step and address any possible issues or questions with students, as well as read the excerpt from the Donald M. Murray book, there is rarely any negativity from my students. The last thing I want is for them to think that the marinating had no authenticity in the process. It did. The marinating that waits patiently for them in their notebooks serves an important purpose, and it will be referred to again, just not right now.

It is important for students to understand that this down draft is not the time to worry about perfection. No one is going to get it right the first time, and they aren't supposed to. The simple act of asking my students to use pencils without erasers helps assure them that it isn't necessary to stop and try to correct during the drafting step. Perfection is not the purpose of the first draft. The purpose is to write and let everything else go away for a little while. One of my favorite authors, Anne Lamott (*Bird by Bird*), helps me get these points across to my students when she says, "Writing a first draft is very much like a Polaroid film developing. You can't—and in fact you aren't supposed to—know exactly what the picture is going to look like until it has finished developing."

As a teacher of writing, I love the sound of the pencils going 90 miles per hour. Nothing gives me more pleasure than observing my students completely engrossed in their writing. This is writing at its best. I find myself just watching my students while they work, which helps me learn more about them as writers. When I am able to experience this free flow of thoughts from my students, I am witnessing the results of my teaching and of my students' acceptance in the role of each step in the drafting stage. It can take a good bit of coaxing and patience for students to succumb to the realization that real writers make mistakes. These mistakes make them better writers. I can pretty much vow to my students that when J. K. Rowling was slaving away on the Harry Potter series, she threw caution to the wind, let the stories emerge, and was comfortable knowing she could fix them up with revision later. These validations, through examples, help my students make these connections. The fact that I have also drafted a piece, right beside them, lets them in on my secrets of the first draft, and it is comforting for them to realize that I make many of the same errors they do. The chart that follows (Figure 6.1, page 128) is a model of the one I give my students before we begin to draft. It is glued in the back of their writer's notebooks and referred to again and again as we continue to draft piece after piece. It gives my students the basic steps of drafting.

## Step Two: The Up Draft

The next step is the "up draft." This is where we reread and fix up our draft by referring back to the marinating in our notebooks. This is not to be confused with revision. It is a simple reference step before the students begin to revise. It often surprises students to realize how much vital information they remembered in the down draft. As they write more and more, this recall of details and facts gets better and better.

**Figure 6.1**    Basic Steps for Drafting

What Am I Doing During the Drafting Process?

I am . . .

1. Closing my notebook and remembering all I can about what I want to write.
2. Writing on YELLOW draft paper.
3. Skipping lines and numbering pages.
4. Writing on ONE side of the draft paper.
5. Focusing on sequence and organization.
6. Continuously writing with a flow of thought.
7. Truly caring about my piece.
8. Being constantly aware of my audience. I do not want them to have questions.
9. Using the entire actual writing time efficiently.
10. Being cautious about my spelling and punctuation.
11. Using a pencil without an eraser.
12. Rereading if I get stuck.

A quote from the movie *Finding Forrester* that I like to share with my students gives them a clear view of what I am trying to convey to them about this step of the drafting stage: "Write your first draft with your heart. Rewrite with your head." So, in essence, the down draft is from the heart and the up draft is from the head—with a chance to refer back to the careful marinating (planning) that took place in the writer's notebook. It is important for students to understand that they may vary from their plan, and that is fine. The plan is just a stepping-stone, and parts may be skipped, added to, or rearranged. This is what the process is all about. I stress to my students that we aren't worried about revising or editing our pieces right now. We simply want to check the structure and sequence and add any additional details that may have been left out. We want to build and inspect our "structural framework," or draft. My students understand that we are about to share with a writing buddy, so as a courtesy to the reader, we want a draft that feels complete—not perfect, just complete enough for someone to get the gist of the author's purpose and be able to compliment the high points the piece has to offer. After a couple of days drafting comes the crucial next step: sharing.

# The Crucial Step of Sharing

It typically takes two days for the drafting process, one for each step in the stage. Students spend one day writing the down draft and one day writing the up draft. On the second day of drafting, after the students have had the opportunity to reread and add important details, it is time to share.

I believe that sharing is crucial in the success of students' writing. In my classroom, we are a community, and all are aboard the same boat we call "writing." I want my students to share after their drafts are completed because it gives them a chance to think out loud and hear their pieces for the first time. It is also good to allow your students to step away from their own drafts before the stage of revising takes place, and sharing is a beneficial way to accomplish this task.

Writing is an act of silence, and there has to be a time to break that silence, throw the fear aside, and trust your fellow writers. To make sure that this trust is instilled, the first time my students share with another, the only feedback they receive is positive. We use a simple "What I liked/Why" T-chart to document the moments in the piece of writing that are worth celebrating. Let me use a conversation I heard between Isaac and Drew to show you what I mean.

**Isaac:** OK, Drew, are you ready to share with me?

**Drew:** Yep, let me just get these pages numbered for you. I can't believe my draft is almost eight pages long.

**Isaac:** Let me grab us a couple of T-charts from the basket so we can get started.

## My Red Light System

At this point, Isaac went where I keep the sharing charts. He knew that the charts in the green basket are for the first share, the charts in the yellow are for the second share, and the ones in the red basket are for the final share. I use the red light system as a visual for my students.

First share: After drafting (This is where Isaac and Drew were.)
Green basket
What I Liked/Why T-chart
- The writer reads aloud the piece while their partner makes notes on the T-chart. Then the roles are reversed. I advise

my writers to stop briefly at the end of each page so their partner can have time to reflect one page at a time.

**Second share:** After revising
Yellow basket
2 Stars and a Wish T-chart
- Writing partners swap pieces and each piece is read silently while the T-chart is being used. The purpose for silent reading is so the partner can find that moment that the writer needs to work on. That is more easily accomplished if the partner can see the text and reread parts.

If you are unfamiliar with the 2-stars-and-a-wish strategy, it simply means that the writing partner gives the piece of writing "two stars," or two compliments. Then "a wish," or a piece of advice, is given.

**Third share:** After editing or right before publication
Red basket
Wows/Wonders T-chart
- During this sharing, the writer and the partner are active participants. The writer reads some parts aloud while the partner may ask to read some silently. Both students, for both pieces of writing, celebrate the moments of "wow" and focus on the moments they may still "wonder" about. I always stress that as writers, we do not want to leave our readers with any unanswered questions. Having a writing partner to "bounce" a story off of, helps build confidence and add any potential information that may have been left out.

**Final share:** After publication
Large sticky note
- This final act of sharing takes place in the author's chair. We all gather around the student writer in our meeting spot and listen as each student writer comes forward to share their published piece. I let the listeners know ahead of time that I may ask them to compliment a word, or a sentence, or a part from the writer's story. After the student writer has read us the piece of writing, I ask for three students to tell something positive or memorable about the piece of writing. I document what is said on a large sticky note. Then I place that sticky on the front of the published piece. This step makes the writer beam with pride but also holds the listeners

accountable. I believe we learn from listening and we gain confidence when complimented. This step takes care of both.

## Our Sharing Charts

On pages 132–133 you will find samples of the three sharing charts that we use—**What I Liked/Why** (Figure 6.3), **Two Stars and a Wish** (Figure 6.4), and **Wows/Wonders** (Figure 6.5). I like to put two on a page and then cut them apart. I find that, even though the space gives students plenty of room to write comments, it isn't as daunting as a full sheet of paper. Plus, if they need more room, they can simply flip it over and write on the back. It is important to also note that these charts are available for students when they begin to self-discover the craft that mentor texts offer. I find this especially true with the **What I Liked/Why** and the **Wows/Wonders** charts. When my students use the Wows/Wonders chart while reading a book they have chosen to research for writing craft, the wonders are not questions that have arisen because the author left out important information, but because it sparked an interest and pushed them to question and then research to find the answers. A wonderful example of this would be with the mentor text *Train to Somewhere*, by Eve Bunting. I read this book earlier in the year as a read aloud. One of my students, Cindy, chose to look back through the book and completed a **Wows/Wonders** T-chart. The evidence of craft is apparent. But Cindy also began to wonder about the real "orphan train." These wonders led her to research, and this research resulted in two separate pieces of writing: a fictional narrative (in a diary form) and an expository essay. A sample of Cindy's chart is provided in Figure 6.2 (below).

**Figure 6.2**   Cindy's Study Chart

| *A Train to Somewhere*, by Eve Bunting | |
| --- | --- |
| *WOWS* | *WONDERS* |
| Reflected in the dirty glass | *the story takes place in 1877 |
| Gliding fast and smooth | *why were 100,000 children homeless |
| Clickety-clack, clickety-clee | *was this a problem only in New York |
| The man is tall and stooped | *Charles Loring Brace |
| "Cor blimey!" | *the "orphan train" |

## Examples of the Sharing Charts

**Figure 6.3**  What I Liked/Why T-Chart

| What I Liked | Why |
|---|---|
|  |  |

**Figure 6.4**  Two Stars and a Wish T-Chart

| Two Stars | A Wish |
|---|---|
|  |  |

**Figure 6.5** Wows and Wonders T-Chart

| Wows | Wonders |
|---|---|
|  |  |

## Picking Writing Partners

I allow my students the opportunity to pick their own writing partners, except for the whole-group sharing time at the end. But I stress that they pick someone different for each sharing opportunity. After each sharing session, the writers keep the T-charts as tools to guide their publication. When a student has published a piece of writing, I ask that all evidence of sharing be stapled to the back of the draft so I can look over them. This is an excellent source of formative assessment. I am able to see not only how specific their partner's responses were but how well the writer is applying the strategies taught in our mini-lessons.

Let's get back to Isaac and Drew and see how their sharing was progressing.

**Isaac:** I have a chart for you and a chart for me. Let's go sit at the back table for our sharing.

**Drew:** Perfect. Would you like to read your piece first? And I will begin filling out the T-chart as you read.

At this point, Isaac was reading his piece aloud. Drew was right there beside him looking over the text while Isaac read aloud. I noticed Drew beginning to document on the T-chart, so I got a little closer to see what he had written. See Drew's work in Figure 6.6 (below).

Two things were happening here. First, Isaac was getting to share his piece and hear how it flows. The flow and rhythm of writing is referred to as sentence fluency. When a student reads aloud, mistakes are often noticed, left out words added, and the young writers notice when sentences are too long and need to be shortened or vice versa.

The second thing that was happening is that Drew was using the language of writers to explain to Isaac why he liked what he liked. There is no vagueness. I teach my students to speak concretely, and I make sure I do as well. This precision is also applied when we study a mentor text or a student's sample of writing. I don't want my students to just tell me they liked the ending of *Owl Moon*. I want them to recognize that the author, Jane Yolen, ended with a feeling and advice. We also infer that when she wrote those final words, "The kind of hope that flies on silent wings under a shining Owl Moon," she realized she had just crafted the title for the book. If Drew had just written "good word choice" for "scampered" instead of "strong verb for movement," Isaac may not have known exactly what craft strategy he used to help his writing. If our students don't know what they did effectively—precisely and concretely—they can't repeat it, and we want our students to repeat the good writing moments. We want students' perceptions of their writing to be based on this type of interaction with other writers (students and the teacher alike), not solely on grades, scores, or judgments.

**Figure 6.6**   Sample of a Sharing Chart

| What I Liked | Why |
|---|---|
| • How you began your story with a setting | *It gives me a visual of where the story takes place |
| • The word scampered | *It's a strong verb for movement |
| • Your use of dialogue in the second paragraph | *Dialogue makes me feel like I am there in the story |

## Making the Most of Sharing

Let me stop here to make sure that I stress to you the importance of modeling these sharing T-charts with your students. I go so far as to put in student examples from previous years in the baskets for additional visuals. Seeing what types of information another student provided to their writing partner helps clarify not only the teacher's expectations but also those of the student writer.

Let's take a closer look at the **"What I Liked/Why"** T-chart that I keep in the green basket. I find that if I begin the year using the **What I Liked/Why** T-chart after each sharing of a mentor text with my students, they begin to become familiar with this way of reading like a writer. We brainstorm the craft and techniques the author used, concrete examples from the book (*what we liked*), and then we discuss *why* these noticings were effective. This type of modeling is vital to students. They need to see how and why these charts can be used and what purpose they serve. This understanding is important because the act of sharing is both objective and subjective. To make sure that my students fully understand the step of sharing I need to

1. lay down all guidelines,
2. fishbowl the procedure,
3. provide models from other students, and
4. walk them through the process with a mentor text.

If I follow these steps accurately then I have paved the road to sharing success. I follow this same procedure for all three of the sharing charts that my students use.

## A Moment to Discuss Writer's Block

There are some writers who firmly believe in writer's block, and there are many who do not. I believe there can be a mental block that can prohibit a writer from writing. I also believe that this block can be worked through and learned from. One technique I provide for my students is what I call "the SAFE method." I give my students a chart that they glue in the back section of their writer's notebooks. If, at anytime, they feel this compulsion to give up or that the task is too great, I invite them to slow down and reread the SAFE chart. It really helps. Just knowing that they have permission to feel a little overwhelmed and that the strategies on the chart may

**Figure 6.7** SAFE Chart

---

### Strategies to Push Past Writer's Block

**S**top and reread

**A**sk yourself questions . . . "What do I need to say? Does my writing connect to my topic?"

**F**reewrite for a few minutes

**E**nergize your draft with new ideas

---

lift this block they are experiencing is beneficial for my students. There is consolation in knowing that they are not alone and that writers get frustrated and freeze up—it's all part of the process. I often share with my students that even Ernest Hemingway said the most frightening thing he ever encountered was "a blank sheet of paper." Figure 6.7 (above) shows that simple SAFE chart.

## Closing Thoughts

I want my students to experience many things during the stages of drafting and sharing. For drafting, I want them to let go of the notion that they are going to get "this thing called writing" right the first time. Stephen King puts it so eloquently, "Only God gets it right the first time." As my students grow as writers, they will begin to find fewer basic errors in structure and sequence. They will also continue to get better at recalling important details that are important for their piece of writing. But the need to reflect and plan never goes away. For sharing, I want them to recognize the sensitivity of a writer and keep this sensitivity in the backs of their minds when working with a writing partner and offering compliments and comments about a piece of writing. It is necessary for students to realize that in order to grow as writers, they must share and be receptive to the comments that may ask them to take a closer look at that piece of writing. Finally, I want my students to have numerous opportunities to share and hear not only positive feedback but careful critiquing. There is a little sign that hangs above my board. It is a gentle reminder during the sharing process. It simply says, "We are partners . . . never targets." And that goes for me the teacher as well. It is my job to guide my students and help them see the potential they have as writers. I must make the workshop a place of safety and show, through my own writing, how to live vicariously through the pencil. I must show that we as a community of writers will share our successes and offer suggestions that will help each of us grow to meet our full potential.

In closing, I would like to share one of my favorite excerpts from Natalie Goldberg's book *Writing Down the Bones*. I share it with my students as well. It reminds us all that writing is hard, and kind words can give a writer that extra nudge they may need.

> "As writers we are always seeking support. First we should notice that we are already supported every moment. There is the earth below our feet and there is the air, filling our lungs and emptying them. We should begin with this when we need support. Begin from these. Then turn to face a friend, and feel how good it feels when she says, 'I love your work.'"
>
> —Natalie Goldberg

## Chapter Seven

# Ideas for Revision

"Good writing happens when human beings follow particular steps to take control of their sentences—to make their words do what they want them to do."

—Ralph Fletcher

## Where Do I Start?

For years I struggled with exactly what to teach my students during the revision stage of the process. There are so many preprinted lessons and ideas on the Internet that I admittedly got swamped by the possibilities. Then, about two years ago, my revision lessons became my own and, more importantly, were purely driven by the needs of my students.

I want to start this chapter with some quotes from writers that I share with my students. These quotes give a framework for what is expected during this stage of the process. I simply write these quotes on sentence strips and display them near the white board.

- "I'm not a very good writer, but I'm an excellent rewriter."
  —James Michener

- "Revision plays a very large role in writing. Sometimes it seems to be all revision. And the longer I write—the more I revise—and it's never completely right."
  —Ellen Hunnicut

- "I love revising but I don't think of it as rewriting. I see it as layering. I keep adding layers to my book, each time concentrating on a different area such as characters, details, plot, description, etc."
  —Ben Mikaelsen

- "A writer needs to 'ache with caring' over a piece of writing."
  —Mem Fox

- "Revision is very important to me. I have to revise, cut, shape. Sometimes I throw the whole thing away and start from scratch."

  —William Kennedy

- "I have rewritten, often several times, every word I have ever published. My pencils outlast their erasers."

  —Vladimir Nabokov

- "For me, revising is part of the whole process. It's learning."

  —Jack Prelutsky

When considering what to teach your students about revision, examples of good writing are great places to start gathering ideas and information. At the beginning of the year, I am training my students to read like writers, and almost every mini-lesson begins with a good book aka mentor text. These mentor texts not only offer the students ideas for collecting possible writing later, but they also give concrete examples of what we look for in good writing. I know that if my students can recognize and discuss what makes writing good, then they can also apply it to their own. It's a basic **(1) notice it, (2) name it, (3) try it, (4) apply it** type strategy. I have signs on my board for these four steps of recognizing and applying quality writing. I want my students to see the constant connection that my lessons have to their own writing and to the process. Figure 7.1 (below) is a sample anchor chart that my students brainstormed about "what makes writing good?"

**Figure 7.1** Sample Anchor Chart

---

### What Makes Writing Good?

- Beginnings that grab the reader
- Endings that leave the reader thinking and reflecting
- Strong verbs
- Similes for the senses
- Dialogue
- Juicy color words
- Voice
- Interesting facts
- Concrete examples; specificity
- Adjectives
- Creative punctuation

---

We added to this list throughout the year when students become even more familiar with the qualities of good writing. This happens when students experience:

1. Mentor texts that are shared
2. Self-discovery of what they like in mentor texts and their own writing and why
3. Publication and self-assessment

It is during the stage of revising that careful examination of these qualities are noticed, named, tried, and applied to a draft.

As I finish reading a mentor text, my students and I begin to talk about the parts of the book we liked and why. We notice everything from the craft to the structure to the conventions. We basically put the mentor text under a microscope or through a sieve. For example, after I read *Owl Moon*, by Jane Yolen, I realized there were numerous moments of greatness or specific craft found within its pages. The chart in Figure 7.2 (page 141) provides a few examples from the book. It is these small moments and parts of writing that we discuss and document under the **Notice It** sign on my board. After we notice what is good about the writing, we name the strategy the author used and put this information on the board under the **Name It** sign. I like to start off by allowing students to simply discuss what they liked with regards to writing style and craft in the book.

I try not to get too bogged down with what to call the specific craft. I want the language to be natural and come from the students. I do try to avoid general terminology (show don't tell, mind movie, word choice) and work with the students to name the craft in such a way that it makes sense to them and can be applied throughout the year. The language of my students will mature the more they hear me speak it and the more exposure they have to naming specific craft.

Each of the examples of craft that we listed on the chart in Figure 7.2 can become a revising mini-lesson for me to teach later. Now, imagine for a moment just how many mini-lessons you can collect if you study what is good about several of your favorite books. The need for tons of preprinted lessons is no longer needed. You have created your curriculum based on the observation of your students and books you are familiar with. This type of studying and collecting keeps your lessons fresh, new, and differentiated. And don't be surprised when your students start bringing you examples from books they may be reading. There is no greater joy for me, as a writing teacher, than to have my students as active participants of a study, reading like writers, and feeling the urge to share this information with others.

**Figure 7.2** A Study of Owl Moon

---

### A Study of *Owl Moon* by Jane Yolen

| *Notice It: Craft/Structure/ Creative Conventions* | *Name It: Strategy Used* |
|---|---|
| • The trees stood still as giant statues. | * Simile for sight |
| • We reached the line of pine trees, black and pointy against the sky. | * Details of setting |
| • My mouth felt furry, for the scarf over it was wet and warm. | * Descriptive adjectives for touch |
| • And when their voices faded away it was as quiet as a dream. | * Simile for sound |
| • For one minute, three minutes, maybe even a hundred minutes we stared at one another. | * Use of time to slow down a moment |
| • Then the owl pumped its great wings and lifted off the branch like a shadow without a sound. | * Simile for sight/strong verb (pumped) |

---

I feel it is important for my students to know that the literal definition of revision means "to see again." We like to use a dictionary to get a formal definition, and then we put it in our own words. Nowhere do those definitions imply that our writing will be perfect after we revise. That is what is so wonderful about writing; we strive for a perfection that isn't supposed to be attained. I love it. And if I keep the "layering" in mind with regards to Ben Mikealsen's quote, I am no longer confused about when and what to teach. I let the needs of my students and the endless examples of craft from mentor texts guide my curriculum. Drafting and revising. You can't do one without the other. Each goes hand in hand with the other. I can't revise a piece I haven't written and I can't write a piece without the hopes of getting a chance to revise it.

## Considering What to Teach

When I conduct workshops for my school district, I often find that the stage of revising is the one that seems to give teachers and ultimately students the most problems. It was a struggle for me at first

**Figure 7.3**  Revising Chart

REVISING is like remodeling a house because you may . . .

1. Knock out a wall (or a paragraph)
2. Join two rooms together (or combine sentences)
3. Put in a new window (or clarify ideas)
4. Sculpt the walls with Spanish lace (or add creativity strategies)

EDITING is the cleaning or straightening up (or fine tuning for the reader and the presentation).

until I allowed myself the opportunity to stop and reflect on the true meaning of the word: "to see again." At that point, I sat down and created an analogy chart that I supply to my students. (See Figure 7.3 above.) The chart gives them a visual to help see the purpose of revising. This chart is glued in the back of their writer's notebooks.

The first time my students revise their drafts I like to focus on various ways they can begin their stories. We understand, at this point in the process, that we must grab our readers. Author Joan Lowery Nixon makes this point well: "Work extra hard on the beginning of your story, so it snares readers instantly." It is my belief that you may not be able to judge a book by its cover, but you can judge a book by its first line. Because we have studied so many mentor texts up until this point, my students have been exposed to numerous brilliant beginnings. It is then my job to review with them the creative ways that Jane Yolen, Eve Bunting, Gary Paulsen, and many other published writers have begun their stories. We study the techniques and determine the strategy used. These "noticings" are written on an anchor chart called "Brilliant Beginnings." Most writers will tell you that you basically have three seconds to grab the attention of a reader, so make it good—and that is our objective with the following lesson.

## Lesson on "Brilliant Beginnings"

### *Step One*

**Me:**  Class, let's look for just a moment at one of our favorite mentor texts, *Owl Moon*. What did we notice about how Jane Yolen begins this story? Let's add the beginning of this story to our ongoing chart of brilliant beginnings we have collected and let's figure out what strategy she used."

**Figure 7.4**   Brilliant Beginnings Anchor Chart

---

**Brilliant Beginnings**

*Owl Moon*, by Jane Yolen
It was late one winter night,
Long past my bedtime, when Pa and I went owling.
There was no wind.
The trees stood still as giant statues.
And the moon was so bright the sky seemed to shine.

---

At this point, I am directing my students to the anchor chart we have on the board. Refer to Figure 7.4 (above).

**Grayson:**   I noticed that she described the setting to start her story.

**Me:**   You are right, she did. What words did she use to let us know this?

**Lily:**   She used *past my bedtime* and that let me know it must be late.

**Me:**   Very good. Is there anything else?

**Susan:**   The words *winter night* let me know the season and time of day and that is important for a setting.

**Me:**   You got it! Is there anything else about the beginning and how she uses the setting to grab our attention?

**Luke:**   I like how she snuck a simile in there, "*The trees stood as giant as statues.*"

**Me:**   I do too. We will look even closer at how to write similes when we revise and try to add a few similes to our drafts.

**Carl:**   Can I add that I already know who the main characters in the story are? Does that count as setting?

**Me:**   Excellent observation. I think it is important to know who is in this setting and what their plans are. In this case, we know right off the bat that Pa and the small child are going owling, at night, in the winter.

### Step Two

My next step for this lesson is to give my students a chance to look back at the beginnings of the narrative drafts they have been working on and see if they can add to or rewrite their beginnings—

making sure to include the setting like Jane Yolen did. This is the **Try It** part of our revising step. Once I have given them time to do this, we share with the class. I typically teach my students two different ways to begin a story on our first journey through to publication. There are over 35 different ways to begin a piece of writing. It is my goal to provide my students four or five options for how to begin a piece of writing within the course of the year. The students discover many more simply through our class studies of mentor texts and their own reading. I want to slow down my revising lessons and achieve a feeling of depth not just coverage.

## Another Sample Lesson

My next revising mini-lesson might involve teaching my students about the use of similes to help give their readers a comparison and ultimately a better mental picture. I want my students to know *why* we are adding the techniques we are adding. If all I say is, "Today we will learn to write a simile," I am not sure my students understand *why* we are learning to write similes and the purpose of adding them to our own drafts. Whenever I teach a revising lesson (or any writing lesson), there are two questions I ask myself to help keep me direct and clear:

1. **What** exactly am I teaching?
2. **Why** am I teaching this?

I must get very specific in my language, and it is my goal for my students to be able to use specific language, too. It is the modeling of this specific language that helps my students identify specific craft as well as the purpose for adding the specific craft. Always clarifying *why* is a great place to start. And why we add similes is to give the reader a visual, usually for one of the five senses, actions, or an emotion.

Let's look at a revising mini-lesson for creating and adding similes. First, I ask my students to look back through the notes we have taken from mentor texts we have studied throughout the year. This information is located not only on anchor charts displayed around the room but also in the back of their writer's notebooks. These notes from mentor texts are collected in the form of the **Notice It/Name It** chart like the one we used for Jane Yolen's book *Owl Moon*. Let's focus on this particular book for this simile lesson example. By the time my students and I were finished studying *Owl Moon*, we noticed 21 examples of specific craft that good writers use and good writing has. Since I have informed my students that we are going to work on creating similes today, it doesn't take them long to hone in on the fact that *Owl Moon* has several examples. The booklist that is provided in the appendix will give you a place to start with your search of specific craft and with turning that study into revising lessons. It is at this point I show students how to write a simile.

## Step One

The first step in creating a simile is to identify the people, places, or things in the draft. I ask my students to circle them. After they have circled several words in their drafts, they create a simple chart labeled "people, places, and things." One student, Alecia, had a list that looked like this:

| People | Places | Things |
|---|---|---|
| Grandmother | Shopping center | Earrings |
| Police officer | Claire's Boutique | .Satin purse |

## Step Two

The next step is for students to think of words that describe those people, places, and things. Alecia's chart began to look like this:

| People | Places | Things |
|---|---|---|
| Grandmother/old | Shopping center/large | Earrings/sparkly |
| Police officer/tall | Claire's Boutique/ crowded | Satin purse/green |

## Step Three

Finally, I ask my students to write down other objects with *similar descriptive words* as the ones they just applied to the chart. So in the end, Alecia was able to create several similes. Here is a look at her final chart:

| People | Places | Things |
|---|---|---|
| Grandmother/old | Shopping center/large/ *football stadium* | Earrings/sparkly/ *diamonds* |
| Police officer/tall/*tree* | Claire's Boutique/ crowded/*church on Easter* | Satin purse/green |

Here are the similes that Alecia was able to create after looking at the Jane Yolen examples from *Owl Moon* and letting me guide her with some basic steps.

- The police officer was as tall as a tree.
- The shopping center was as large as a football stadium.
- The earrings were sparkly like diamonds.
- Claire's Boutique was as crowded as my church on Easter morning.

Note that Alecia couldn't think of any similar descriptive words for the grandmother or the satin purse, and that was fine. Alecia went on to add all of the new similes to her existing draft. When I conferred with her about this lesson, she was able to tell me that the similes she wrote and chose to add to her draft gave the reader a comparison for sight. This showed me she knew *why* she was asked to take this revising step, and that gave the mini-lesson purpose.

## Brainstorming Mini-Lessons for Revising

I do not get my mini-lessons from a year-long curriculum, but rather I choose them based on the qualities of good writing and my favorite picture books. I also like to use and study my students' writing, as well as my own, to brainstorm what it is I want to teach them and what I am noticing they need to work on during revising. I literally sit down and ask myself, "What do I want to teach my students that will make their writing better? I make a list of these and put a simple box out to the side. When I introduce a lesson, I add a date to the box, and when I reintroduce a lesson, if needed, than I add another date to the box. Here is a small sample of that list.

### Mini-lessons for revising:
- Similes
- Brilliant beginnings
- Exceptional endings

- Onomatopoeia
- Alliteration
- Sensory details
- Adding action to dialogue
- Strong verbs
- Metaphors
- Breathtaking adjectives
- Adding emotions
- Slowing down a moment (We call this the "hover moment." I have also seen it referred to as the "hot spot.")
- Changing the tone of the writing
- Changing the point of view
- Changing the tense (from past to present or future)
- Adding or deleting a part*

*I often use the analogy of the rose bush to help my students see the purpose of "cutting" some of the unnecessary parts in their writing: "A rose bush grows healthier after it is pruned."

Another helpful hint is to show students the **A.R.R.R.** method:

**A**dding: What else does the reader need to know?

**R**earranging: Is the information in logical the most logical and effective order?

**R**emoving: What unnecessary bits of information are in this piece of writing?

**R**eplacing: What words or details could be replaced for clearer or stronger expressions?

This is not all I teach my students about revising within a year, but I hope it gives you an idea of where to start. Revising is about:

- Fixing up writing and adding some creativity to the piece
- Exchanging overused words for those with more punch
- Getting rid of what may not be needed and focusing on what is
- Adding details that will make meaning clear for the reader
- Adding action and emotion to the hover moment

Again, remember the house analogy I shared at the beginning of the chapter:

- Knock out walls (or paragraphs)
- Join two rooms together (or sentences)
- Put in new windows (or clarifying ideas)
- Sculpt the walls with Spanish lace (or add creativity skills)

# The Hover Moment

Let me take a minute to go over what we refer to as "the hover moment." All good stories have a rising and falling action. They also have a beginning, a middle, and an end. What we refer to as the hover moment is where the story takes a turn for either the better or the worse. It is the top of a roller coaster you are about to do down. The rising action of the story got you to the top, and it is there you will stay for a while to hone in on details, emotions, and important events. It is the purpose for the piece. I enjoy using the book *Dog Breath*, by Dav Pilkey, to show my students exactly what I mean. If you aren't familiar with the beginning of the story, it is about a dog with really bad breath. The family tries everything to help the poor pooch but nothing is working. In the middle of the story, burglars come in to rob the house. The dog startles the would-be robbers and ultimately saves his family. The family awakens to see the robber passed out from the horrific fumes of the dog's breath. That whole scene is the hover moment. It is that moment when things begin to change in the story, and in this case for the better. In other words, the reader is provided with a frame-by-frame detailed description of what is happening in this crucial point in the story. The end of the story, or falling action, is simply that the dog becomes a hero, and the family decides they can't live without him. I spend several days showing students different examples of hover moments from books we have read and studied.

# Tying Books into My Revising Mini-Lessons

Let's look again at that list of mini-lessons on pages 146–147. I want to take it a step further, and brainstorm books that would fit in nicely with these lessons. Again, the booklist you will find at the back of the book will help you get started. As you study your own favorite books, you will hopefully begin to feel more comfortable with the process, become knowledgeable about many new books, and add to the lists that I have provided. Please note that, because the examples I am about to show you are in the extensive booklist (page 191), I will not add authors' names to this mini-lesson chart.

### Mini-lessons for Revising:
- Similes: *Owl Moon; Crazy Like a Fox*
- Brilliant beginnings: *Owl Moon; The Harmonica*
- Exceptional endings: *The Hat; Smoky Night*

- Onomatopoeia: *Click Clack Moo: Cows That Type*; *The Noisy Book*
- Alliteration: *The Great Fuzz Frenzy*; *Six Snowy Sheep*
- Sensory details: *Night in the Country*; *Miss Rumphius*
- Adding action to dialogue: *The Keeping Quilt*; *The True Story of the Three Little Pigs*
- Strong verbs: *Brave Irene*; *The Everglades*
- Metaphors: *Twilight Comes Twice*; *The Whales*
- Breathtaking adjectives: *The Important Book*; *Roller Coaster*
- Adding emotions: *How Are You Peeling?*; *Old Black Fly*
- Slowing down a moment (the hover moment): *Dog Breath*; *Old Yeller*, p. 113
- Concrete details (specificity): *Goodnight Moon*; *Chrysanthemum*

## A Guide to Keep You Organized

On the next page is a sample chart that I use to organize my mentor texts and decide when I want to use them with regards to revising. I keep this chart handy while I am studying my mentor texts and add titles to it as I go. This chart is never far from my side because my students often offer me examples of specific craft from their own reading, and I want to be ready to grab that information and add it to my chart. About two weeks ago, I was approached by one of my students. She was holding a chapter book in her hand. She was beaming with excitement to share with me how she had discovered that the first page of her new book contained a description of a setting, a simile, and several strong verbs. I immediately asked for permission to make a copy of that page as well as the cover of the book so I could use it in future mini-lessons. This student is learning how to read like a writer, and I couldn't be prouder. I rushed to the copy room, made the necessary copies, and added the title of her book to my list like the one I am providing in Figure 7.5 (pages 150–151).

## A Final Note

When we ask our students to revise, we are asking them to do what real writers do. Revision is important, and a concise and clear plan of action helps give our students a necessary foundation. When we use quality mentor texts to help our students see what good writ-

**Figure 7.5** Mentor Texts for Revising Mini-Lessons

| Mini-Lesson | Mentor Text | Mentor Text | Mentor Text |
|---|---|---|---|
| Brilliant beginnings:<br>• Setting<br>• Problem<br>• Character<br>• Flashback | | | |
| Exceptional endings:<br>• Lesson learned<br>• Solution<br>• Circular<br>• Memory | | | |
| Strong verbs | | | |
| Adding attributes:<br>• Size<br>• Color<br>• Shape<br>• Texture | | | |
| Similes for:<br>• Sight<br>• Sound<br>• Taste<br>• Touch<br>• Smell<br>• Emotions<br>• Actions | | | |
| Dialogue + Action | | | |
| Onomatopoeia:<br>• Soft sounds<br>• Loud sounds<br>• Scary sounds<br>• Funny sounds | | | |
| Hyperbole | | | |

**Figure 7.5** (*continued*)

| Mini-Lesson | Mentor Text | Mentor Text | Mentor Text |
|---|---|---|---|
| Idioms | | | |
| Alliteration | | | |
| Describing the setting with:<br>• Attributes<br>• Descriptive language<br>• Time of year/day<br>• Time period | | | |
| Adding sensory details to writing:<br>• Sight<br>• Smell<br>• Touch<br>• Taste<br>• Hearing | | | |
| Focusing on the hover moment by:<br>• Adding dialogue<br>• Slowing down (frame by frame method)<br>• Adding action<br>• Adding emotion<br>• Showing the reader rather than telling | | | |
| Breathtaking adjectives | | | |
| Adding emotions:<br>• Positive emotions<br>• Negative emotions | | | |

ing is, that foundation is strengthened. It is important that, during revision, students do not view this stage of the process as only one where mistakes are found. Rather this stage of the process is one where they have the opportunity to see their writing in a new way and take something that that wasn't and make it so. There is a genuine sense of satisfaction when a piece of writing feels complete.

## Chapter Eight

# Polishing, Publishing, and Portfolios

*"Be lavish and abundant with your words. Let yourself go in first drafts and learn to come back to your writing with a calmer, more careful editing eye."*
—Naomi Nye

## The Final Frontier

Publication is not the sole purpose for writing, but it does make the writer feel complete. It gives my students a chance to polish, publish, and present. It is a moment of celebration and reflection on all that has been accomplished and the hard work put forward.

## Polishing Up by Editing

I tell my students that one of the main reasons writers edit is as a courtesy to the reader. If you have ever read a paper that was filled with spelling and mechanical errors (and I am quite sure you have), you know the frustration it presents. I need my students to feel the potential frustration that someone reading their paper may feel if they don't take one last look and edit. I have a slew of "non-examples" of good writing that I refer to as anchor papers. I allow my students time to take a closer look at these before we take the next step. Here are a few comments that I often hear.

- "Ms. Morris, the handwriting is so bad I can barely read it."
- "There are like 40 misspelled words in this story."

- "I can't believe it! There is not one period in the entire paragraph. . . . I needed to breathe."
- "I found myself very confused because sometimes the story was in the present and then the past and then the future."

When students study good writing, they learn what is expected, and when they study poor writing, they also learn what is expected. These anchor papers serve us well in all stages of the process. Once this activity has been completed and our findings have been discussed, it is time for me to show my students how to edit their own papers. Again, I stress that I am not striving for perfection; it is just important for them to take that last moment of review to polish what they have written so they can be proud of their writing and the reader can be entertained or informed.

Editing is layered. Like each step of the writing process, it has many steps and purposes. Sometimes writers edit for *formal publication* and sometimes for *informal publication*.

## Formal Publication

A few examples of formal publication are:

- Bulletin board display
- School newspaper
- Contest

When a student publishes formally, the standards for finding and correcting errors are higher. Students should spend a little more time on editing and ask a peer editor to double-check their paper.

## Informal Publication

When I refer to *informal publication*, I am considering the publications for a portfolio, a writer's notebook entry, or a letter to a friend. The editing is still relevant, but the time spent on this stage may be lessened. It is important for students to conduct an efficient yet effective scan of a piece of writing in which they target a few specific areas. My fourth-grade students are given a standardized writing test. During this test, they have 45 minutes to plan, write, and edit. That's it. I want them to focus more on the content of the piece of writing then the mechanics.

# Areas for Editing

It makes the stage of editing a little easier if students see it as a series of steps rather than a whole process. These steps may include:

**Capitalizing:** titles, proper nouns, beginning of sentences

**Punctuating:** sentences, dialogue, possession, creative uses (ellipses, semicolons, hyphens, and dashes)

**Spelling:** checking a word wall, using a dictionary, sight words

**Grammar:** keeping tense uniform (past, present, future), subject and verb agreement

**Presentation:** spaces between words, neat handwriting, indenting new paragraphs, and appropriate margins

# Proofreading Marks

I do not mandate that my student s use formal editing marks. I always provide them with a reference chart of the basic marks, display an anchor chart with the same information, and encourage the use of the marks. But sometimes a student may simply circle a word that needs to be checked for spelling accuracy. If they remember to put the *sp* part of the editing mark, that is great, but if not, that is OK as well. My goal is for them to recognize and correct their errors. Figure 8.1, below, is a sample chart I provide my students. It is glued in the back of the writer's notebook.

**Figure 8.1** Basic Editing Marks

| Make a capital letter | we ate a yummy pizza yesterday. |
| Make a lowercase letter | We ate a yummy Pizza yesterday.   lc |
| Add a period | We ate a yummy pizza yesterday ⊙ |
| Delete | We ate a yummy pizza yesterday. |
| Use correct spelling | We eight a yummy pizza yesterday. |

**Figure 8.2**  Student Editing Checklist

---

**Student Editing Checklist**

**Title of Writing**_____

**Date**_____  **Author**_____

**Directions: Use the questions below to evaluate your paper. Make the corrections needed as you go.**

1. Did I write my name on my paper?
2. Does my paper have a title?
3. Do I begin each sentence with a capital letter?
4. Did I end each sentence with the correct mark?
5. Did I spell the Word Wall words correctly?
6. Did I indent each paragraph?
7. Does my first sentence catch my reader's attention?
8. Does my last sentence finalize my purpose or point?
9. Are my sentences complete thoughts?
10. Did I use my best handwriting?
11. Did I pay careful attention to the subject/verb agreement?

---

## A Student Checklist

I find it helpful to give my students an editing checklist that helps them evaluate and correct their drafts. Figure 8.2 (above) shows that checklist.

## Helpful Hints

Checklists are very important to provide for your students, but so are helpful hints. Here are just a few.

1. **WAIT!** If possible, wait a day or two before you begin to edit your piece of writing. Sometimes stepping away for a little while will help you see errors more clearly.
2. **Read it Backward.** Although this sounds a little silly, it really works. Start at the end of your piece of writing and concentrate word by word until you get to the beginning. This trains your eyes to catch the mistakes because you are focused on individual words.

3. **Begin in the Middle.** Another excellent way to edit is to begin in the middle of your piece of writing. Go through the middle to the end and then from the beginning to the middle.

4. **Keep Writing Tools Handy.** Make sure you have a dictionary, sight-word cards, and your hand available for this helpful hint. Remember that after you trace your hand, label each finger with five areas you are targeting.*

*Hands Up for Editing*
*To teach students this method of editing, all you need is a hand. Have the students trace their open hand on a blank piece of paper, and write on each finger what they are looking for when they edit their writing. One finger is for capitalization, one finger is for neatness, one finger is for spelling, one finger is for punctuation, and one finger is for subject. The point of the last finger, staying on subject, is to help prevent students from writing something off topic.*

5. **Read s-l-o-w-l-y.** Lots of important editing moments can go unnoticed when you read too fast. Take your time. Think of editing as a detective would a mystery case, and don't leave one sentence unsolved.

## Acronyms for Editing

There are numerous acronyms out there that are quick and easy editing tools for students. I have these examples posted around the room, and my students can use whichever one is needed at the moment. I particularly like the GUMS, COPS, and CUPS checklists shown in Figures 8.3, 8.4, and 8.5 (page 158). We simply use sticky notes and write the acronym on a sticky note for an easy and efficient method of editing. The line outside of each letter is provided for students to put a check beside the specific area once it has been edited.

## Thoughts on Spelling

One of the first areas of editing that I cover with my students is spelling. I find with my fourth graders that many of the misspelled words in a draft are due to habit. The students are capable of selecting the correct way to spell the word from a list or a mentor text, but lack the strategic background knowledge to figure

**Figure 8.3** GUMS Checklist

**GUMS**

**Grammar** _____

**Usage** _____

**Mechanics** _____

**Spelling** _____


**Figure 8.4** COPS Checklist

**COPS**

**Capitalization** _____

**Organization** _____

**Punctuation** _____

**Spelling** _____


**Figure 8.5** CUPS Checklist

**CUPS**

**Capitalization** _____

**Usage** _____

**Punctuation** _____

**Spelling** _____

out the correct spelling on their own. The following techniques have helped my students identify and correct the necessary words.

- Circle any suspicious words that look wrong.
- Read one of your circled words slowly and stretch it out.
- Write the letters for the sounds you hear.
- Read the word again. Be sure you have a letter for each sound.
- Use the first-try/second-try strategy*
- Don't let tricky words trick you. Be careful with homonyms, homophones, and words with prefixes and suffixes.
- Use other resources: dictionary, spellchecker, peer editor, student-created spelling list

*For this editing strategy, I simply ask that the students create a tricolumn chart in the back of the writer's notebook and then use the above techniques to help them correctly spell the circled words in their draft. I do not expect that every word that is circled must be spelled correctly, but I do ask that my students get as close as they can. The tricolumn chart gives me that evidence that I need, and it provides my students a place to practice. It is important that they try to spell the words correctly by themselves before going to the dictionary or other resource for a final attempt. For the section we label "OK," the student either puts a check mark representing that he was successful in his attempts to spell it correctly or writes in the correct spelling after using a dictionary. Figure 8.6 (below) is an example of what that chart looks like.

**Figure 8.6**   A Sample Chart for the First-Try/Second-Try Method

| First Try | Second Try | OK |
|-----------|------------|-----|
|           |            |     |
|           |            |     |
|           |            |     |
|           |            |     |
|           |            |     |

## Points to Remember

When it comes to editing, there are a few points that I need to keep in the back of my mind, and I would like to share them with you.

**Remember:**
- Do **not** hold students accountable for correcting things they have not been taught.
- Do **not** expect students to spend days correcting errors.
- **Do** expect them to learn the proofreading process and find and correct **some** errors.
- **Do** make sure your editing expectations are grade-level appropriate.

## Publishing and Celebrating

I believe that Lucy Calkins sums up the point of publishing when she says, "Our children will regard themselves in a dramatically new light if they are published authors. Because publication can provide such perspective and tap such energy, I believe it must be one of the first priorities in our classrooms."

The word *publishing* means "to make public," and there are countless ways to publish. I do not believe that publication has to be elaborate or take a great deal of time. After all, the real purpose of writing is the process, but publication does offer a genuine experience for our students. Here are just a few ways to celebrate writing and go public:

1. Meet in writing groups where all students share their pieces aloud.
2. Place the published pieces on desks and tables and let students walk around and read the different pieces. You can have sticky notes handy so that the reader may give the writer a compliment.
3. Put all of the writing together in a class book, and display this masterpiece in your class library.
4. Share with other classes. This is always a favorite activity.
5. Create a bulletin board that highlights student work.
6. Make the writing into gifts.
7. Send student writing to magazines or contests.

# Resources for Children's Writing and Publishing

There are countless ways to publish student writing. One of my favorites (and one of my students' favorites) is submitting their work to magazines and contests. Here are a few places that accept children's work:

## Online Resources

*Young Writers Online*   *Young Writers Online* is *Young Writer*'s sister electronic edition. *Young Writer* (paper edition) is an international magazine featuring the best in English language creative writing by children ages 6 to 16 from around the world. Fun, instructive, and designed to build any child's confidence, *Young Writers Online* is a forum for young people writing fiction and nonfiction, prose and poetry.

*Scriptito's Place*   This is especially for young people ages 7 to 15. Vangar publishes things by young people to show other young people that they can do it too.

*Kidworld Magazine*   A collection of puzzles, stories, and other good things.

*MidLink Magazine*   An electronic magazine created by kids, for kids in the middle grades, generally ages 10 to 15. Browse the interactive space to enjoy art and writing that will link middle school kids all over the world.

*InkSpot*   A large and rich resource on writing and publishing for young people.

*The Young Writers' Club*   This club aims to encourage children of all ages to enjoy writing as a creative pastime by getting them to share their work and help each other improve their writing abilities.

*Young Writers' Clubhouse*   Created by Deborah Morris, the author of the Real Kids, Real Adventures series. This site offers a great deal of sound information and many opportunities for young people through writing.

*The Diary Project*   The Diary Project is a way for young people around the world to share their personal thoughts, feelings, and dreams with one another near and far via the Internet. They can ask questions and find answers about growing up at the turn of the 21st century.

*KidNews*   This is a free news and writing service for students and teachers around the world. Anyone may use stories from the service for educational purposes, and anyone may submit stories. They also invite comments from students and teachers about news gathering, teaching, and computer-related issues.

*Kidpub*   More than 10,000 stories written by kids from all over the planet!

*Kid Space*   This site was launched in March 1995 as a personal home page at Interport Communications. The site rapidly developed and now has many sections, including creative-activities communication pages and sections for learning basic computer skills. The site has generated a worldwide following with readers from over 115 countries.

*The Mighty Pen (On-Line Magazine)*   *The Mighty Pen* is an online magazine is made by and for young adult writers. It features poems, short stories, essays, articles, reviews of concerts, music, movies, and books, accompanied by graphics and pictures.

## *Magazines*

*Children's Playmate* (ages 5–8)
P.O. Box 567B
Indianapolis, Indiana 46206

*Cricket* (ages 6–12)
P.O. Box 300
Peru, Illinois 61354

*Highlights for Children* (ages 2–11)
803 Church Street
Honesdale, Pennsylvania 18431

*Jack and Jill* (ages 8–12)
P.O. Box 567B
Indianapolis, Indiana 46206

*Stone Soup* (ages 5–14)
P.O. Box 83
Santa Cruz, California 95063

## Supplies for the Publishing Center

It is important for teachers to establish a designated area where students can go to publish. This area should house everything that may be needed. Here is a sample of the items I have available for my students in our publishing center.

- Yarn or string
- Magazines
- Envelopes
- Scissors
- Sponges for painting
- Long-arm stapler
- Glue
- Wallpaper books
- Tape, both clear and colored
- Fabric pieces
- Markers, crayons, colored pencils
- Decorative hole punchers
- Standard hole punchers
- Copy paper, both colored and white
- Glitter
- Construction paper
- Stickers
- Plastic page protectors
- Watercolors
- Brads and silver O-rings

This list should get you started, but don't be surprised when your students offer suggestions that can help you as well.

## Self-Reflecting on Writing

At the end of each unit of study, when the writing has been published, students should reflect on what they have learned as writers. There are two ways I do this. The first is as a whole group. We gather at our meeting spot prepared to share with each other what we have learned. I am usually standing at the board—chart paper and pen ready to record comments. This is a great way to introduce the concept of self-reflecting. The students learn from each others' comments and are better prepared when, the next time they reflect, you ask them to record their reflections in their portfolios. Our portfolios are made using manila folders. I store all of the portfolios in hanging folders and place them in a milk crate. I make sure that they are accessible to my students. Feeling ownership of the portfolios is essential in helping students see themselves as writers. Let's take a moment to look at the purpose of portfolios.

## Process and Product Portfolios

It is important for teachers to introduce portfolios at the beginning of the year. I like to send home a letter explaining the purposes and processes associated with portfolios. I also explain that most of their child's published pieces will remain in the portfolios, but that parents are welcome to come and enjoy their child's writing at any time. Figure 8.7 (below) is a sample of the letter that I send home.

**Figure 8.7**   Sample Letter

Dear Parents,

Just like you, I want to make sure that your child is able to make the most of our writer's workshop this year. One of the tools we will be using is a portfolio.

Throughout the year, your child and I will select and insert pieces of writing into the portfolio. The purpose of the portfolio is to assist students in observing progress made over the course of the school term and/or year. I want your child to feel ownership in his or her literary works.

By using a portfolio, your child has assumed the responsibility for learning how to self-reflect and to self-evaluate pieces of writing. This awareness of one's self as a writer is critical in setting individual goals for future growth. The use of portfolios also gives me, the teacher, a better understanding of your child's thoughts and values on writing.

Because of the importance these portfolios hold in our writer's workshop, I ask that they remain in the classroom until the end of the year. Please know that you are welcome to view the writing samples in your child's portfolio at any time. I look forward to having the opportunity to sit with you and discuss our writing goals and objectives this year.

Thank You,

Ms. Morris

# Recording Sheets

It doesn't take long for the portfolios to begin to fill up with student writings. It is important that students keep them somewhat organized as a courtesy to me, their parents, and their fellow writers. I have a simple recording sheet that my students place inside their portfolios. Whenever a new piece is added, the date, title and any comments are recorded in what we call "A Portfolio Summary." Figure 8.8 (below) shows a blank version of a Portfolio Summary, and Figure 8.9 (page 166) shows a student's version.

**Figure 8.8**  A Portfolio Summary

| Name: _____ Date _____ | |
|---|---|
| **DATE** | **TITLE/COMMENTS** |
| | |
| | |
| | |
| | |
| | |
| | |
| | |
| | |
| | |
| | |
| | |
| | |

**Figure 8.9** Student Sample of Portfolio Summary

(Note that the student's errors have been retained for authenticity.)

Name: _____ Date: _____

## A Portfolio Summary

| Date | Title/Comments |
|------|----------------|
| 9-23-08 | Personal narrative |
| 9-15-08 | Grandparants day |
| 9-8-08 | Labor day |
| 9-29-08 | The signs of Fall |
| 10-6-08 | Johny Appleseed day |
| 10-13-08 | Star spangled banner |
| 10-27-08 | Exopsitory |
| 10-27-08 | The Importance of eating healthy |
| 11-14-08 | Haunted house |
| 10-27-08 | Fav. Relative |
| 10-21-08 | Neighborhood playground |
| 9-11-08 | 911 |
| 11-20-08 | Wood babies |

## A Little More About Self-Reflection

Earlier, I covered how my students become comfortable with self-reflecting as a whole group. The time does arrive when they need to go a little deeper. This is where the self-reflecting in the portfolio comes into play.

About six times a year, I ask my students to select a piece of writing and reflect on what they did well and what they need to work on. I have a list of questions that they keep in their portfolios to help jump-start evaluating their own work.

- Why did I write this piece? Where did I get my ideas?
- Who is the audience and how did it affect this piece?
- What skills did I work on in this piece?
- Was this piece easy or difficult to write? Why?
- What parts did I rework? What were my revisions?
- Did I try something new? What?
- What evidence of writer's craft enhanced my piece of writing?
- Did something I read influence my writing?
- What did I learn or what did I expect the reader to learn?

I ask students to fill out a reflection sheet like the one in Figure 8.10 (below). A student example is shown in Figure 8.11 (page 168).

**Figure 8.10**  Our Self-Reflection Sheet

|  | **What I Learned About Being a Writer** |
|---|---|
| Project # |  |
| Project # |  |
| Project # |  |
| Project # |  |
| Project # |  |
| Project # |  |

**Figure 8.11** Student Sample of Self-Reflection Sheet

(Note that the student's errors have been retained for authenticity.)

| N = Naritive    E = Exopistory    FC = Free Choice | |
|---|---|
| **What I Learned About Being a Writer** | |
| Project #1 (N) | Thers alot of procesess taken to prepare for the story. I could really put in alot of dialoge and find ways to make my story bettr whith word choice. I had alot of trouble whith spelling and will be sure to try wen harder whith it. |
| Project #2 (E) | You realy do have to work hard and sweet and think outside the box you have to be willing to look for juicy words and keep trying and It will pay off By time!!! |
| Project #3 (FC) | Sometimes Being Independent can help you but its also hard to let go of help. You have to keep beiliving you can do it and cant fall back. If you want to wright on a project make sure you know what your wrighting about! You just always ALWAYS make sure you know what your wrighting about first! I bet I could have scored a six if I knew what I was. |
| Project #4 (N) | I learned from this project that being locked in a school can be trrifying! Serriosly though. I learned to put A Huge punch of Emotion. |
| Project #5 (E) | I learned Here that sometimes youre orignall ideas dont work Because you cant get enough Details and I learned the Formula for a perfect expository pararaph. |
| Project #6 (FC) | W.O.W! What else is there to say?! The exprience was Awsome and I could remeber everything so clearyly this story was soooo much fun to write! |

Writers read like writers. That is the goal for our students. We want them to see themselves as writers—because they are. By taking the time to reread a published piece, my students gain insight on what worked and what didn't. That is learning and independence at its best. As teachers, we need to see inside the minds of our students. We need to know what they are feeling and how much they gained from a unit of study. We need this information to drive our curriculum and allow us to plan for future instruction. If a simple portfolio paired with some type of reflection sheet can achieve this, and it will, then we have ended our journey through publication with a feeling of success. That is what keeps our writers wanting to write more and more.

## Chapter Nine

# Conferencing with Confidence

"By truly listening to students when we confer, we let them know that the work they're doing as writers matters."

—Carl Anderson

I met Daniel several years ago. He was taller and bigger than the other students, and Daniel hated to write. Each day was a struggle for him to put any words on paper, and his disposition was one of failure. The other students in my class were throwing caution to the wind and writing page after page, but not Daniel. It didn't take long for me to decide that my conferencing sessions with him should be centered on conversations about his life. It is hard to conference with a student that has no writing to show you. I needed to get Daniel writing, and the conversational approach worked. Daniel was free with his stories, verbally, and soon realized that he could salvage these stories, and grow as a writer, if he simply put them on paper. And that is what he did. Pretty soon Daniel was writing on his own and our conferences took on a more curricular approach.

## What Is a Writing Conference?

A writing conference is a conversation about a piece of writing in progress. It is the time for the teacher to listen to the student writer. Some teachers dread conferences because they put too much emphasis on what questions they are supposed to ask. The good news is there are no magic questions. One of the best books I have read on conferencing is Carl Anderson's *How's It Going?* This basic question he asks his students at the beginning of each conferencing session opens up of conversational and curricular opportunities. It is important for teachers to note that the conference is not the time to fix everything in a piece of writing. It is a time for the teacher to reflect on the good parts of the writing and provide feedback for one small moment that can help the writer—not just for one piece of writing but for all future writing pieces of writing as well. When I first added the component of conferencing to the writing workshop, I admit that I probably offered too many of my own ideas and forgot that it was the student's writing not mine. I soon realized that I needed to back away and make sure that all students felt the ownership of their own writing and that this ownership provided the opportunity for independent learning. If I constantly told my students how to improve their writing, then I was handicapping their ability to figure out, like real writers do, the parts that needed to be left alone and the parts that needed to be worked on.

## Purposes of a Writing Conference

Donald Graves summed up one of the real purposes of the writing conference when he said, "When I confer with you about your writing, you are more important than the writing." Our students need to know we value them as writers. This is one factor that makes conferencing such an effective teaching tool. The other factor is the opportunity to teach based on the individual needs of each writer. That is powerful teaching. The writing conference provides the teacher the chance to:

- Listen to the writer. Our schedules are hectic and our teaching time is jam-packed. A writing conference gives me a chance to know my students better on an individual basis. Each snippet of writing I read or they read to me lets me into their world and their thoughts. This is valuable information.
- Confirm what the student is doing well, how effectively my mini-lessons have been taught, and how effectively the student is applying the information from the mini-lessons to writing. I always make a big deal when I come across a piece of writing where the student has practiced the mini-lesson for that day. I give that student the opportunity to share at the end of writing workshop that small moment of instruction they captured in writing that day.

- Assess any confusion or strengths. It is important that I, the teacher, make myself constantly aware of what my students are doing well and what they may still be struggling with. If I see several students struggling with the same concept, I can pull them together for a group conference and save some valuable time. It is also important that I know what my next steps will be, and the conference provides me with this information.
- Set goals with my students. I want my students to become independent writers, and the conferences give them the confidence necessary to continue to move forward. I will get into the structure of my conferences later, but an important component of a writing conference is to start with a strength and then build upon that strength. When a teacher highlights a student's strength, the student becomes more open to hearing more about an area of craft that needs work and setting personal goals to focus on this area.

## Types of Writing Conferences

There are many different types of conferences that a teacher or student can use, and each type of conference serves a particular purpose.

### Whole–Class Sharing

Whole-class sharing is an informal type of conference where all of the students are listening and giving positive feedback to the writer. We gather at our meeting area for these conferences, and the writer sits in the author's chair. I like to record the compliments or suggestions that the other students make on a large sticky note. Then when the conference is finished, I give the comments to the writer to be used later during independent writing.

### Quickshares

A quickshare is simply that. Students are asked to pick one line or one small section from a piece of writing, and we simply go around the room sharing out loud. I will often ask one or two students to briefly comment after each writer shares. This type of conference usually occurs at the end of writer's workshop. My students love this type of conferencing because they thrive on sharing and get excited when asked to locate that one small exceptional moment in their writing.

## Self-Conferencing

I like my students to be independent thinkers and writers. I provide them with a self-assessment checklist that helps them ask questions of themselves. This is a good way for students to consider what is going well and what concerns exist. Here are some examples of questions on the checklist:

- Is my topic clear?
- Did I use enough details?
- Are the punctuation and capitals used correctly?
- What creativity skills did I use? (alliteration, simile, personification, etc.)
- Is my conclusion interesting?

## One-on-One Formal Conferences

At a one-on-one conference, I am sitting with one student and focusing on one piece of writing. What we are discussing depends on where the student is in the writing process. Most of my anecdotal notes come from the one-on-one conference. In this kind of conference, I am focused on a strength, asking guiding questions, and then teaching a skill, strategy, or technique. This is the type of conference that most teachers seem to be familiar with.

## Roving Conferences

A roving conference is what I refer to as a "conference on the run." I also refer to this as my seven minutes of research. It gives me the chance to assess the room quickly and determine the status of the class before deciding which student or group of students I will confer with first. I take notes if I see a student who is distracted or hasn't progressed through to the next step in the process for several days. This may be the student I want to focus on first when it's time for the one-on-one conferences, which usually follow the roving conference.

## Peer Conferences

When I ask students to come together and share pieces of writing, I want them both to walk away from the experience having gained from it. In Chapter Four, I discussed several T-chart methods that are used during sharing. These same charts can be used during a peer conference, which is basically what we consider the sharing step in the writing process. I stress that students need to focus on praising just as much as they do polishing. The types of charts my students use during a peer conference include the following:

- Wows/Wonders
- What I Liked/Why
- Three Stars/A Wish

### Small-Group Conferences

There are times that I am able to group students together and teach one particular skill that needs to be addressed. I form these small group conferences based on my findings from either the one-on-one conferences or my roving conference. It is during group conferences that I am able to utilize much of my conferencing time. I like to have no more than five students in a group conference.

### Process Conferences

A process conference is based on what step a student is at in writing process. I will break down how I conference within each step later. I like to look at each step in the process as a separate curricular opportunity. I know that all steps of the process merge together to reach the goal of publication, but there are so many subskills within each step that it helps me to look at them individually when I conference. I want to teach students to be aware of their own writing process. In this conference the teacher allows students to voice their strategies.

### Evaluation Conferences

After I have scored a published paper, I sit down with each student and go over the strengths, the weaknesses, and some suggested strategies for improving those weaknesses. I use my anecdotal form when I assess and even let the student see my notes. I want my students to understand why they scored what they scored, strategies I would like to see them repeat on the next paper, and of course some areas to improve.

# When Do I Conference?

I confer with individual students or small groups of students during the independent writing part of our workshop. Since 50 percent of our workshop time is devoted to independent writing, I have at least 30 minutes a day to confer. For teachers who have less than a 60-minute writing workshop your time for conferences will be less. The beauty of small-group conferencing can be a lifesaver for the teacher who only has 30 or 45 minutes set aside each day for writing workshop. Each individual conference is typically five to seven minutes long, so I can usually confer with four or five students in a class period. If I can also pull together a group conference, then I can maximize my time even more.

# The Structure of a Conference

When I conference one-on-one, I like to move around the room. I put my conferencing apron on and grab my clipboard. On my clipboard I attach record-keeping forms that help me keep track of each student's progress. During a conference I like to sit next to a student with the piece of writing between the two of us. It is easy for me to determine the stage of the process a student is in by the supplies I see the student using. If yellow drafting paper is out and a pencil without an eraser, I know the student is drafting. If I see a blue pen I know that revising is taking place, and a red pen would be my sign that the student is editing. That information alone helps me to narrow down my curricular options. This doesn't mean that if a student is in the editing stage but then wants more help with a brilliant beginning (this is where drafting or revising typically comes in) that I will only focus on an area of editing. Knowing where a student is in the process is a nice guideline, but conferences are based on the needs of the writer. In his book *How's It Going*? Carl Anderson helps identify three steps that a teacher can take during the first part of a conference.

## Step One

Ask an open-ended question. Some examples of open-ended questions are "How's it going?" and "What are you doing as a writer today?" These type of questions invite students to open up and tell you what they're doing and where they may need help.

### Step Two

Ask follow-up questions. I do not believe that teachers need to walk around with a list of questions or comments on ready-made lists or flip charts. I find that the best questions come naturally and from the writing. I like to ask my students what strategies they used in this particular piece of writing and if they discovered anything about themselves as a writer by working through the process. I enjoy hearing about the moments in the writing that made a student feel successful and the moments that made the student struggle. And if I have a personal connection to anything the student says, I share it as well.

### Step Three

Look at the student's writing. I cannot determine an area of need or an area of strength if I do not take a moment to look at the piece of writing. If we are working on a unit of study on personal narratives and I have focused several mini-lessons on brilliant beginnings, I will look closely at this part of the student's writing. It is important that I stress here that before I address any area of need with a student, I will first compliment something the student did well in the writing. I want this praise, as well as the area of need, to be explicit and never vague. If I tell a student, "You have nice word choice," I can assure you this student isn't clear on what I am saying. If, however, I look at the student's paper and say, "The strong verbs *drifted* and *devoured* in the opening sentence grabbed my attention and made me want to read further," the student understands the value and impact that these two words made on me, the reader. It is important to capture, inspire, and teach during a conference. It is also important to make students aware of their strengths as well as of areas that need improvement.

## Conferencing Throughout the Process

During the first two weeks of school, when routines are being established and writing stamina is increasing, my conferences are more like more conversations, very similar to the example I gave with Daniel's story. I am trying to get to know my students on a more personal level. I ask questions regarding likes and interests. My anecdotal notes are filled with personal snippets of information that I can use later. For example, if Jon tells me he has three golden retrievers, then I want to make a note of this. Then the next time I am sharing funny stories about my Labrador retrievers, I can look to Jon and ask if his dogs have done similar things. It's about forming trust and a community where we each get to know each other. Teachers and students spend a lot of time together, and I want to know my students and I want them to know me. Our schedules are so jam-packed each day that it is a welcome treat to sit beside one student or a small group of students and just share. I have found that conferences, if started in this low-key manner, are not intimidating to students. Seeing me walking around wearing my conferencing apron and carrying a clipboard brings out excitement in the students, not dread.

## My Conferencing Apron

There are several tools I need when I sit down to have a conference with a student or a group of students. Several years ago, I was shopping at my local Home Depot and noticed that their famous orange aprons were on sale—so I bought one. I immediately thought of filling it with supplies I use daily in a writing conference. My apron holds the following items:

### Sticky Notes (Several Sizes)

I like having sticky notes handy to write down what areas of strength and what areas of need are discussed. This gives the student a reminder of our conversation. I have found that students like to keep these inside their notebooks for future reference. I typically make my notations on my anecdotal page on a clipboard.

### Red Pen

When my students edit their writing they use a red pen, but I do not edit a piece of writing during a conference. If during a conference, however, I notice that an area of need is an editing issue, I like the student to use the red pen to practice the targeted skill we have just gone over. For example, if I am sitting with a student who has several examples of proper nouns without a capital letter, I obviously want to address this. On the back side of a draft or a salvaged practicing page in the notebook, I will model the correct way to address a proper noun and then have the student use the red pen to practice doing the same.

### Blue Pen

The use of the blue pen is much like the use of the red one, except we use blue for our revising skills. So if I find a student is beginning each sentence with the same word, I will ask them to brainstorm additional ways to begin sentences and then allow them to fix up their piece of writing with the blue pen. In Chapter Seven I covered a variety of strategies that I teach during the revising process. The checklist of mini-lessons for revising can be copied and used during conferences as well.

### Stickers/Stamps

I may teach fourth grade, but my students still smile big and wide when I give them a little reward sticker or stamp. Sometimes I will give a student a sticker during a conference or during my seven minutes of research before conferencing begins. Remember, I walk around the first seven minutes of independent writing time to observe my students and give them a little time to write before I begin to conference with them. When I see a child diligently working then I will quietly slip over and put a sticker or stamp on the page they are working on. I do not have a set routine or number of days per week I reward this way. It's just another tool in my conferencing apron that I can use when I want to.

I also like to carry around the small self-inking stamps that Oriental Trading or your local Dollar Tree usually have available. The seasonal ones are always fun to use and the students get excited about this little reward system.

### Did-It Dots

Another reward system that works well with my students are the "did-it dots." Real writers set daily goals for themselves of a certain number of words of pages. To help inspire my students to push themselves a little bit further, I assign a certain number of pages I feel should be written during independent writing. At the beginning of the year, I typically require one page a day minimum, but as the year progresses that requirement can and does grow to as much as four or five pages a day. The last five minutes of independent writing time I simply walk around and ask the students to show me their assigned number of pages, and I put a did-it dot in the corner of their paper. The did-it dots are those small round stickers that teachers use for basic goal setting charts. It doesn't take long for me to train several reliable students to help me in this process of giving out did-it dots. Again, it is just a small little token of appreciation I give to my students for working hard each day. I feel it is important to point out that I do differentiate the number of pages for some of my struggling writers. If the class has worked themselves up to four pages a day then there may be a few students whose three pages would require just as much effort. This is a very relaxed system that I use and that is the beauty of it. It is between me and the writer and about recognizing growth and hard work.

### Conferencing Compliment Cards

As with the stickers and stamps, I like to have a flexible way to reward students who are working diligently. It's another great way to motivate students who might be having a hard time focusing or getting started for the day. Once the other students see that I am passing out conferencing compliment cards it's magical the way they sit up straight and work extra hard. The same happens when they see me passing out the stickers and stamps. I keep a variety of cards in my apron and after a conference I like to give the student I have just worked with a verbal compliment as well as a card. I find that my students like to glue these cards on the front or back cover of their notebooks. I have even seen some students collect them like baseball cards and see how many they can accumulate each nine weeks.

## The Collecting Step

After the initial two weeks of school, I have started my collecting lessons. My conferences are now geared more towards helping my students fill their charts with seed ideas. It often takes a little coaxing to help students realize that they have had many experiences that they can write about. As scientist Linus Pauling once said, "The best way to have a good idea is to have lots of ideas." Many teachers in my school still use prompts as a main way to motivate their students to write. So when students come to my classroom, it feels a little different when they are asked to look closer at their lives. I will admit that there are moments when I think it would be easier just to give my students prompts, but the essence of the writing that I see when I teach them to look deeper and closer at the small moments in their lives is definitely worth the extra effort. I find that gathering several students together for a group conference can help generate memories that can be written about. Conferencing at this step may look to an outsider like a writing group huddled together at Starbucks on a Saturday afternoon. The goal is to collect ideas and to bounce those ideas off of other writers for feedback. And this is what real writers do.

## The Selecting Step

After several mentor texts have been read and charts in the back of the notebooks have been filled with ideas that may make the journey through to publication, it is time to select and narrow down the possibilities. In Chapter Four, I covered the step-by-step questioning process that I use to help students make this selection. My conferences now take on a whole-group questioning- style prompting. Once each student has selected an idea to write about, I call the class to the front. Many teachers forget how valuable whole-group conferencing can be. It is important for students to have the opportunity to use their voices and share their ideas. This is the perfect time for this type of instruction. After the students gather at the meeting area, I ask individual students to tell the group their ideas for the upcoming piece of writing. Each child gets this opportunity. I put each of the ideas on a large sheet of chart paper, with the student's name beside it, and this chart is displayed on the board until we have published the pieces. But I don't stop there. I ask questions to prompt details and make sure that other students can ask questions as well. Each student has two to three minutes to tell us about the idea that was selected. It typically takes me two days to get through this process, but it is well worth it because our next step is marinating, and this sharing opportunity has been a "safety stop" along the way, just like the marinating step will be. It is important that once a student starts to draft a paper, they are committed to that idea.

## The Marinating Step

Planning is critical to organizing thoughts. When my students come to me at the beginning of the year, I often find that the sequence and organizational patterns in their writing are very hard to follow. It is this exact reason that I began to slow down the steps to publication and added the marinating step. I have found two very effective ways to conference during this step.

## Formal Conferences

A formal conference is a one-on-one conference where I am looking closely at the organizational plan a student has completed. If we are studying narrative writing, a student may have chosen a B/M/E column chart (Beginning, Middle, and End) to organize events in the story. I am not looking at conventions or spelling or word choice. I am looking at structure. Here is a sampling of teachable moments I may look for:

- Title
- Grouping of like ideas
- Sequence of events in a logical order
- Transition words
- Time order words
- Topic sentences

Again, during the marinating step, my conferences are focused on structure and what fits within that structure.

## Small Group Marinating Conferences

If, during my seven minutes of research, I find several students who seem to be having a hard time marinating on (planning) their topics, I ask them to come to my table. I have photocopied and laminated some of my favorite planning organizers and these are used to help students who are struggling. I provide each student in my group with a wet erase pen and a laminated organizer. As a group we briefly discuss each student's topic or idea. Then I ask the students to plan, not in their notebooks, but on the laminated organizers. I like for them to plan one section at a time. Let's go back to the B/M/E chart I was referring to earlier. I would ask for only the beginning to be planned, and then I would give it a quick check. Next, we would concentrate on the middle, and so forth. I admit that this type of conference can take up to 10 minutes, but I am working with about five students at one time so it doesn't keep me from being able to conference individually with the other students who may not need my assistance with marinating.

# Revising and Editing Conferences

The steps of revising and editing are packed with strategies and teachable moments. It is these two areas where most teachers find themselves conferencing most of the time. When I conduct workshops for my county, I often ask teachers to make a quick list of what skills and strategies they focus on during a conference. Here is a sample of what is typically on these lists:

- Spelling (editing)
- Strong verbs (revising)
- Dialogue (editing)
- Punctuation (editing)
- Use of commas (editing)
- Describing words—adjectives (revising)
- Onomatopoeia (revising)

You can see that the areas of revising and editing are what I call comfortable areas, meaning that the skills and techniques that fall within these two steps are recognizable to most teachers. I would suggest that if the skills associated with the revising and editing steps are unfamiliar, then having the list of mini-lessons from Chapters Seven and Eight may help a teacher know what areas to target. Also, remember what mini-lessons you have taught so far. If you haven't taught a mini-lesson on strong verbs, you may wait and conference with a student on the skill after discussing it in a lesson.

# Anecdotal Records

It is important to document during a writing conference. Writing conferences help the teacher assess student progress over time and plan for future instruction. If I walk around and find that a large majority of my students are struggling to remember to start sentences with capital letters, I may want to revisit that skill as a whole-class mini-lesson. Keeping anecdotal notes also allows teachers to group students together who need to work on similar skills. I keep all of my anecdotal notes in a binder. I have four classes of students so I have four different colored binders. I simply put a divider between the students' names for easy reference. There are countless organizers that can be used for anecdotal notes, but the one I use works not only for conferencing but also for assessment. The form shown in Figure 9.1 (below) is attached on my clipboard as I walk around and conference. I use this same form when I am scoring papers. You will notice that the *strength* is listed first because I want to remind myself to look for something the writer has done well. I use the word *weakness* in the next column not as a negative but as a teachable moment. This shows me what I need to focus on with this student or with several students. The *strategy used* column is for me to document how I taught a student the specific skill from the weakness column. The reason I like to document the strategy I used to teach a skill is to make sure I am keeping my strategies fresh and differentiated. It took me several different tries before I came up with the one I am currently using.

## Questions to Consider During a Conference

Every conference will be different, but the following questions can help teachers get the conference going:

- What stage of the process are you in?
- Tell me about your pieces of writing.
- Read me your favorite part of your story.
- What do you need help with?
- I like the way . . .
- How are you creating a mind picture for the reader?
- Why did you choose this topic or idea?

**Figure 9.1** Strengths and Weaknesses Table

| Name | Strength | Weakness | Strategy Used |
|------|----------|----------|---------------|
|      |          |          |               |

## Closing Thoughts

Students will not fall apart and consider themselves poor writers if they know that their work is valued. Teachers have a responsibility to speak to students openly and honestly about their writing. I make a point to emphasize that we are all partners in this community of writers and never targets. In order to grow as writers, however, we must be willing to accept constructive criticism and learn new strategies daily. It is a necessary component of growth and independence. The more opportunities I have to work one-on-one with a student or with a small group, the more layered and differentiated the understanding of writing and the multiple skills necessary to write are addressed. I want my students to have productive conferences with other students as well as with themselves. Ultimately a writer is his or her own reader, critic, and editor. This independence can be achieved through constructive and effective conferences.

# References

Anderson, Carl. *How's It Going? A Practical Guide to Conferring with Student Writers*. Portsmouth, NH: Heinemann, 2000.

Buckner, Aimee. *Notebook Know-How: Strategies for the Writer's Notebook*. Portland, ME: Stenhouse, 2005.

Bunting, Eve. *Fly Away Home*. New York: Clarion Books, 1993.

Calkins, Lucy. *The Art of Teaching Writing*. Portsmouth, NH: Heinemann, 1994.

Culham, Ruth. *6+1 Traits of Writing: The Complete Guide, Grades 3 and Up*. New York: Scholastic, 2003.

Fletcher, Ralph. *Boy Writers*. Markham, Ontario: Pembroke, 2006.

_____. *The Writer's Notebook: Unlocking the Writer within You*. New York: HarperCollins, 2003.

_____. *Writing Workshop: The Essential Guide*. Portsmouth, NH: Heinemann, 2001.

Goldberg, Natalie. *Writing Down the Bones*. Boston: Shambhala, 1986.

Graves, Donald. *A Fresh Look at Writing*. Portsmouth, NH: Heinemann, 1994.

Hale, Elizabeth. *Crafting Writers K–6*. Portland, ME: Stenhouse, 2008.

King, Stephen. *On Writing*. New York: Simon and Schuster, 2000.

Lamott, Anne. *Bird By Bird*. New York: Pantheon, 1994.

Levoy, Myron. *Alan and Naomi*. New York: Harper and Row Junior Books, 1977.

Murray, Donald M. *A Writer Teaches Writing*. 2nd ed. Boston: Heinle, 2003.

Pentacoff, Elizabeth Koehler. *The ABC'S of Writing for Children*. Sanger, CA: Quill Driver Books, 2003.

Pilkey, Dav. *Dog Breath*. New York: Scholastic, 1994.

Ray, Katy Wood. *What You Know by Heart*. Portsmouth, NH: Heinemann, 2002.

_____. *Wondrous Words: Writers and Writing in the Elementary Classroom*. Urbana, IL: NCTE, 1999.

Routman, Regie. *Writing Essentials*. Portsmouth, NH: Heinemann, 2005.

Seuss, Dr. *The Lorax*. New York: Random House, 1971,

Spandel, Vicki. 2004. *Creating Writers Through 6 Trait Writing Assessment and Instruction*. 4th ed. Boston: Allyn and Bacon, 2004.

White, E. B. *Charlotte's Web*. New York: Scholastic, 1952

Woodson, Jacqueline. *Coming On Home Soon*. New York: G. P. Putnam and Sons, 2004.

Yolen, Jane. *Owl Moon*. New York: Philomel Books, 1987.

_____. *Welcome to the Greenhouse*. New York, NY: Scholastic, 1993.

# Quotes from Authors

(organized by stage of the writing process)

## Practicing

"Fill your paper with the breathings of your heart."

—William Wordsworth

"I set myself 600 words a day as a minimum output, regardless of the weather, my state of mind or if I'm sick or well."

—Arthur Hailey

"Writing is the inking of our thinking."

—Robin Fogarty

"Add to the list of topics, in your notebook, anytime you think of something. Then when you sit down to write, you can just grab a topic from that list and begin."

—Natalie Goldberg

"Your writing is trying to tell you something. Just lend an ear."

—Joanne Greenberg

"Love the writing, love the writing, love the writing . . . the rest will follow. "

—Jane Yolen

## Collecting Ideas

"If you breathe, if you live, you have something to write about."

—Donald Graves

"In writing, there is first a creating stage—a time you look for ideas, you explore, you cast around for what you want to say. Like the first phase of building, this creating stage is full of possibilities."

—Ralph Waldo Emerson

"I carry a notebook with me everywhere. But that's only the first step. Ideas are easy. It's the execution of ideas that really separates the sheep from the goats."

—Sue Grafton

"The best time for planning a book is when you're doing the dishes."

—Agatha Christie

"When I am looking for an idea, I'll do anything—clean the closet, mow the lawn, and work in the garden."

—Kevin Henkes

"How to generate writing ideas, things to write about? Whatever's in front of you is a good beginning."

—Natalie Goldberg

"And above all, watch with glittering eyes the whole world around you because the greatest secrets are always hidden in the most unlikely places. Those who don't believe in magic will never find it."

—Roald Dahl

"Actually ideas are everywhere. It's the paperwork, that is, sitting down and thinking them into a coherent story, trying to find just the right words, that can and usually does get to be labor."

—Fred Saberhagen

"Bring ideas in and entertain them royally, for one of them may be king."

—Mark Van Doren

"Begin with 'I remember.' Write lots of small memories. If you fall into one large memory, write that. Just keep going."

—Natalie Goldberg

# Marinating

"To steal ideas from one person is plagiarism; to steal from many is research."

—A. Felson

"In writing, there is first a creating stage—a time you look for ideas, you explore, you cast around for what you want to say. Like the first phase of building, this creating stage is full of possibilities."

—Ralph Waldo Emerson

"What is written without effort is in general read without pleasure."

—Samuel Johnson

"A story should have a beginning, a middle, and an end . . . but not necessarily in that order."

—Jean-Luc Godard

"Man will turn over half a library to make one book."

—Samuel Johnson

"After all these many books, I still over-research."

—Ann McGovern

"Of course it's true, but it may not have happened."

—Patricia Polacco's grandmother

# Drafting

"Quantity produces quality. If you write only a few things, you're doomed."
—Ray Bradbury

"Don't get it right, just get it written."

—James Thurber

"The beautiful part about writing is that you don't have to get it right the first time, unlike, say, a brain surgeon."

—Robert Cormier

"Lower your standards and keep writing."

—William Stafford

"If I waited for perfection, I would never write a word."

—Margaret Atwood

"The faster I write the better my output. If I'm going slowly, I'm in trouble. It means I'm pushing the words instead of being pulled by them."

—Raymond Chandler

"One of the most difficult things is the first paragraph. I have spent many months on a first paragraph, and once I get it, the rest just comes out very easily."

—Gabriel García Márquez

# Revising

"The writer takes the reader's hand and guides him through the valley of sorrow and joy without ever having to mention those words."

—Natalie Goldberg

"A metaphor is like a simile."

—Author unknown

"Rereading reveals rubbish and redundancy."

—Duane Alan Hahn

"Writing is rewriting. A writer must learn to deepen characters, trim writing, intensify scenes. To fall in love with the first draft to the point where one cannot change it is to greatly enhance the prospects of never publishing."

—Richard North Patterson

"The pleasure IS the rewriting. The first sentence can't be written until the final sentence is written."

—Joyce Carol Oates

"The great thing about revision is that it's your opportunity to fake being brilliant."

—Will Shetterly

"Good writing is essentially revision. I am positive of this."

—Roald Dahl

# Sharing

"I am thrilled by children's reactions to my books. That's what fuels me to write other books."

—Marc Brown

"Sometimes you look at your work on the drawing board, and it's like a battlefield. You are fighting to get the picture to turn out right."

—Barbara Cooney

"Writing is a struggle against silence."

—Carlos Fuentes

# Editing

"When you catch an adjective, kill it. No, I don't mean utterly, but kill most of them—then the rest will be valuable."

—Mark Twain

"I can never seem to start writing a book until I know what the title will be."
—Phyllis Reynolds Naylor

"Clutter is the disease of American writing. We are a society strangling in unnecessary words, circular constructions, pompous frills and meaningless jargon."

—William Zinsser

"Words should be weighed, not counted."

—Jewish folk saying

"A synonym is a word you use when you can't spell the other one."
—Baltasar Gracián

"I try to leave out the parts that people skip."

—Elmore Leonard

"Proofread carefully to see if you any words out."

—Author unknown

"If a word in the dictionary were misspelled, how would we know?"
—Steven Wright

# Presentation

"The writing process is hard work and I always look forward to drawing the pictures."

—Marc Brown

"How do you present your papers? As a golden gift on a platter? Or a stinky three day old fish?"

—Donald Murray

"I derive so much pleasure in looking. I hope children will too."

—Lois Ehlert

# Lists of Mentor Texts

(organized by teaching topic)

## Adjectives

Cleary, Brian P. *Hairy, Scary, Ordinary: What Is an Adjective?*
———. *Quirky, Jerky, Extra-Perky: More about Adjectives.*
Dahl, Michael. *If You Were an Adjective.*
Ehlert, Lois. *Fish Eyes: A Book You Can Count On.*
Fleming, Denise. *In the Small, Small Pond.*
———. *Lunch.*
Fleming, Maria. *The Bug Book.*
Fox, Mem. *Tough Boris.*
Fox, Mem, and Judy Horacek. *Where Is the Green Sheep?*
Frazee, Marla. *Roller Coaster.*
Heller, Ruth. *Many Luscious Lollipops: A Book about Adjectives.*
Henkes, Kevin. *Chrysanthemum.*
Lester, Helen. *A Porcupine Named Fluffy.*
Martin, Bill, Jr., and John Archambault. *Chicka Chicka Boom Boom.*
Noble, Trinka Hakes. *The Day Jimmy's Boa Ate the Wash.*
Rylant, Cynthia. *Long Night Moon.*
Schaefer, Lola M. *This Is the Rain.*
Stone, Jon. *The Monster at the End of This Book.*
White, E. B. *Charlotte's Web.*
Wood, Audrey. *Quick as a Cricket.*
Wood, Don, and Audrey Wood. *Piggies.*

## Alliteration

Arena, Felice. *Sally and Dave: A Slug Story.*
Barrett, Judi. *Things That Are Most in the World.*
Base, Graeme. *Animalia.*

191

Berenstain, Stan, and Jan Berenstain. *The Berenstains' B Book.*
Brown, Margaret Wise. *The Important Book.*
Carle, Eric. *"Slowly, Slowly, Slowly," Said the Sloth.*
Crews, Donald. *Cloudy Day Sunny Day.*
Crunk, Tony. *Railroad John and the Red Rock Run.*
Edwards, Pamela Duncan. *Dinorella: A Prehistoric Fairy Tale.*
———. *Some Smug Slug.*
Enderle, Judith Ross, and Stephanie Gordon Tessler. *Six Snowy Sheep.*
Fleming, Denise. *In the Small, Small Pond.*
———. *In the Tall, Tall Grass.*
Frasier, Debra. *Miss Alaineus: A Vocabulary Disaster.*
Hopkinson, Deborah. *Apples to Oregon: Being the (Slightly) True Narrative of How a Brave Pioneer Father Brought Apples, Peaches, Pears, Plums, Grapes, and Cherries (and Children) across the Plains.*
Johnston, Tony. *The Harmonica.*
Kim, Grace. *She Sells Seashells: A Tongue Twister Story.*
Kirk, David. *Miss Spider's ABC Book.*
Martin, Bill, Jr., and John Archambault. *Chicka Chicka Boom Boom.*
Moulton, Mark Kimball. *The Annual Snowman's Ball.*
Palatini, Margie. *Bedhead.*
———. *The Three Silly Billies.*
Sayre, April Pulley. *Vulture View.*
Seuss, Dr. *The Cat in the Hat Comes Back.*
———. *How the Grinch Stole Christmas!*
———. *One Fish Two Fish Red Fish Blue Fish.*
Schotter, Roni. *The Boy Who Loved Words.*
Stevens, Janet, and Susan Stevens Crummel. *The Great Fuzz Frenzy.*
Van Allsburg, Chris. *The Z Was Zapped: A Play in Twenty-Six Acts.*
Wood, Audrey. *The Napping House.*

## Onomatopoeia

Brett, Jan. *The Gingerbread Baby.*
Brown, Margaret Wise. *The Noisy Book.*
Crews, Donald. *Shortcut.*
Cronin, Doreen. *Click, Clack, Moo: Cows That Type.*
Fleischman, Paul. *Joyful Noise: Poems for Two Voices.*
Fleming, Denise. *In the Tall, Tall Grass.*
Fox, Mem. *Night Noises.*
Greene, Rhonda Gowler. *Barnyard Song.*
Hutchins, Pat. *Good-Night, Owl!*
Janeczko, Paul B. *Dirty Laundry Pile: Poems in Different Voices.*
Keats, Ezra Jack. *The Snowy Day.*
Lester, Julius. *John Henry.*
Martin, Bill, Jr., and John Archambault. *Barn Dance.*
———. *The Ghost-Eye Tree.*

————. *Listen to the Rain.*
Munsch, Robert N. *Mortimer.*
Polacco, Patricia. *Thunder Cake.*
Pulver, Robin. *Punctuation Takes a Vacation.*
Seuss, Dr. *The Cat in the Hat.*
Showers, Paul. *The Listening Walk.*
Silverstein, Shel. *Where the Sidewalk Ends.*
Spier, Peter. *Crash! Bang! Boom!: A Book of Sounds.*
————. *Gobble, Growl, Grunt.*
Steig, William. *Brave Irene.*
Weatherby, Brenda. *The Trucker.*
Williams, Linda. *The Little Old Lady Who Was Not Afraid of Anything.*
Yolen, Jane. *Owl Moon.*

# Beginnings

Allard, Harry. *The Stupids Die.*
Brett, Jan. *Berlioz the Bear.*
Bunting, Eve. *Going Home.*
Carle, Eric. *Pancakes, Pancakes!*
Clement, Rod. *Grandpa's Teeth.*
Cooney, Barbara. *Eleanor.*
————. *Miss Rumphius.*
DePaola, Tomie. *The Art Lesson.*
Fleischman, Paul. *Weslandia.*
Gibbons, Gail. *The Honey Makers.*
Gray, Libba Moore. *My Mama Had a Dancing Heart.*
Henkes, Kevin. *Chrysanthemum.*
Hoffman, Mary. *Amazing Grace.*
Hofsepian, Sylvia A. *Why Not?*
Houston, Gloria. *My Great-Aunt Arizona.*
Howard, Elizabeth Fitzgerald. *Aunt Flossie's Hats (and Crab Cakes Later)*
Koralek, Jenny. *The Boy and the Cloth of Dreams.*
Luthardt, Kevin. *Peep!*
Noble, Trinka Hakes. *The Day Jimmy's Boa Ate the Wash.*
Penn, Audrey. *The Kissing Hand.*
Pinckney, Andrea. *Duke Ellington.*
Polacco, Patricia. *Some Birthday!*
————. *Thunder Cake.*
Rylant, Cynthia. *When I Was Young in the Mountains.*
Spurr, Elizabeth. *A Pig Named Perrier.*
Thayer, Ernest Lawrence. *Casey at the Bat.*
Yorinks, Arthur. *Louis the Fish.*
Zagwyn, Deborah Turney. *The Pumpkin Blanket.*

# Endings

Abells, Chana Byers. *The Children We Remember*.
Asch, Frank. *Just Like Daddy*.
Battle-Lavert, Gwendolyn. *The Barber's Cutting Edge*.
Bunting, Eve. *Fly Away Home*.
———. *Smoky Night*.
Bruchac, Joseph. *The First Strawberries*.
Burningham, John. *Hey! Get Off Our Train*.
Cecil, Ivon. *Kirby Kelvin and the Not-Laughing Lessons*.
Cooney, Barbara. *Miss Rumphius*.
Dupasquier, Phillippe. *Dear Daddy*.
Fox, Mem. *Harriet, You'll Drive Me Wild!*
Freeman, Don. *Dandelion*.
Hesse, Karen. *The Cats in Krasinski Square*.
Hoffman, Mary. *Boundless Grace*.
———. *Henry's Baby*.
Joosse, Barbara M. *I Love You the Purplest*.
Kroll, Steven. *The Biggest Snowman Ever*.
Littlesugar, Amy. *Tree of Hope*.
Marshall, James. *Willis*.
McSwigan, Marie. *Snow Treasure*.
Paterson, Katherine. *Bridge to Terabithia*.
Polacco, Patricia. *John Philip Duck*.
———. *Some Birthday!*
———. *Thunder Cake*.
Tsuchiya, Yukio. *Faithful Elephants: A True Story of Animals, People, and War*.
Van Allsburg, Chris. *The Stranger*.
Woodson, Jacqueline. *Sweet, Sweet Memory*.

# Strong Verbs

Aylesworth, Jim. *Old Black Fly*.
Berger, Melvin. *As Big as a Whale*.
Brett, Jan. *The Mitten*.
———. *Town Mouse, Country Mouse*.
Cannon, Janell. *Stellaluna*.
———. *Verdi*.
Cherry, Lynne. *The Armadillo from Amarillo*.
Cleary, Brian P. *To Root, to Toot, to Parachute: What Is a Verb?*
Cronin, Doreen. *Click, Clack, Quackity-Quack: An Alphabetical Adventure*.
Crunk, Tony. *Railroad John and the Red Rock Run*.
Fleming, Denise. *In the Small, Small Pond*.
Fletcher, Ralph. *Twilight Comes Twice*.
George, Jean Craighead. *The Everglades*.
Hesse, Karen. *Come On, Rain!*

Jenkins, Steve. *Move!*
Kellogg, Steven. *Mike Fink: A Tall Tale.*
Krauss, Ruth. *The Happy Day.*
Lester, Julius. *John Henry.*
Pfister, Marcus. *The Rainbow Fish.*
Polacco, Patricia. *Oh, Look!*
———. *Rotten Richie and the Ultimate Dare.*
———. *Thunder Cake.*
Ryder, Joanne. *Won't You Be My Hugaroo?*
Rylant, Cynthia. *When I Was Young in the Mountains.*
Sendak, Maurice. *Where the Wild Things Are.*
Steig, William. *Brave Irene.*
Tucker, Kathy. *The Seven Chinese Sisters.*

# Sensory Details

Ball, Jacqueline A. *Riddles about the Senses.*
Brown, Margaret Wise. *The Noisy Book.*
———. *The Seashore Noisy Book.*
Cole, Joanna. *You Can't Smell a Flower With Your Ear!*
Cooney, Barbara. *Miss Rumphius.*
DePaola, Tomie. *The Popcorn Book.*
Fletcher, Ralph. *Twilight Comes Twice.*
Guiberson, Brenda Z. *Into the Sea.*
Hall, Kirsten. *Animal Hearing.*
———. *Animal Taste.*
Heller, Ruth. *Many Luscious Lollipops.*
Martin, Bill, Jr., and Eric Carle. *Polar Bear, Polar Bear, What Do You See?*
Mathieu, W. A. *The Listening Book: Discovering Your Own Music.*
Pallotta, Jerry. *The Yummy Alphabet Book.*
Paulson, Gary. *Hatchet.*
Ryan, Pam Muñoz. *Hello Ocean.*
Rylant, Cynthia. *In November.*
———. *Night in the Country.*
———. *The Old Woman Who Named Things.*
Showers, Paul. *The Listening Walk.*
Stojic, Manya. *Rain.*
Wallace, Karen. *Think of an Eel.*
Wilson, Karma. *Bear Snores On.*
Wood, Douglas. *A Quiet Place.*
Yolen, Jane. *Owl Moon.*
Young, Ed. *Seven Blind Mice.*